HOME-
DESIGNED
HIGH SCHOOL

By Diana Johnson

Home-Designed High School
published by Home-Designed Schooling
© 2001 Diana Johnson
First published 1996
All Rights Reserved
ISBN: 0-9710734-0-6

Disclaimer: The intent of this book is to provide *ideas and suggestions* for planning a high school course of study. It is up to parents and students to adjust the information presented in *Home-Designed High School* in order to meet the legal requirements for home schooling in their location and to plan a program that best meets their needs. Following suggestions in this book cannot guarantee the success of a home school program or its sufficiency for further academic or career goals. In addition, because life is full of changes, no guarantee concerning the ongoing accuracy of address information can be made.

Available at:
your local Christian bookstore
or from:
Home-Designed Schooling
P.O. Box 133044
Tyler, TX 75713-3044
e-mail: djohnson@thescroll.org

ACKNOWLEDGMENTS

It's amazing how much effort goes into writing a manual — even a short one like this. It's only fitting to mention those who have helped me bring this to completion.

Thank you:

to our Lord and Savior, Jesus Christ. Every blessing and meaningful accomplishment in life is a gift of His grace. *May the beauty of the Lord our God be upon us, and establish the work of our hands for us; yes, establish the work of our hands* (Psalm 90:17).

to my husband John for once again patiently enduring life with me while I was trying to write. Your love, enthusiasm, and pitch in and do the dishes helpfulness kept us all sane!

to my five children Brian, Cara, John Aaron, Grace, and Hannah who have blessed me with a cheerful interest in "mom's book" while adapting uncritically to the haphazard household management that accompanied its creation.

to Marty Barbieri, Dana Bertino, Mary Boner, and Bamma Godeaux for your willingness to proofread my work and the many helpful suggestions that resulted from your efforts.

to the home school moms who shop at the Scroll. You uplift our spirits and lighten our steps with your positive comments. Our casual conversations in the home school aisles have helped refine the Scroll's home school department.

to David for your creativity in this current project and your vision that resulted in the Scroll's home school department. It is truly a blessing to us.

Final Note

I had to make a determination whether to refer to a teenage home school student as *he, she,* or *he/she*. Because I am a traditionalist, the student will be called *he* throughout. Should you think it represents a *she* prejudice on my part, three of my five children (not to mention myself) are females! For balance and to best represent the most common home school situation, I will refer to the home educating parent as *she* when a personal pronoun is required.

Contents

WHY THIS GUIDE WAS WRITTEN

This guide was written as a service to our home school customers at the Scroll Christian Bookstore where, over the last seven years, I have worked part-time developing a home school department. Since writing this guide five years ago, I have had the opportunity to revise it several times, keeping in mind the needs of our home school customers and the needs I had as a home school mom myself. I had several distinct goals in mind each step of the way.

Because home school moms are busy people, I desired:

- to make the guide as user-friendly as possible.
- to present the information in a simple, step-by-step format.
- to keep record keeping to a minimum.

Because each home school family is unique, I desired:

- to make the method adaptable to different approaches to learning.
- to provide sample classes but encourage personal creativity.

Because our lives are not our own, I desired:

- to encourage each home school to excel for the good of all home schoolers.
- to encourage excellence to bring glory to God.

Our customer comments have been encouraging, which led me to make this guide available to a wider audience. Now, I hope it will be helpful to you.

INTRODUCTION

The title of this book is *Home-Designed High School*. *Home-designed* means personally planned education by the parents and student to best meet the needs of their situation. Each of our home schools looks and operates differently. Often our plan changes significantly from one student to another. Yet guidelines are needed that encourage academic excellence and purposeful life preparation without unnecessarily hampering the wonderful flexibility and freedom of home schooling. It is my hope that this book will offer a reasonable structure within which creativity and individualized education can flourish.

As you consider the suggested guidelines, realize that they do not represent absolutes. Some of my ideas may not work for you. I do not have your wisdom and insight into the needs of your family and individual students. I have different state regulations than you have. I encourage you to interact with my thoughts, adapt them freely, and plan the program that seems best for you.

Over the last eighteen years of home schooling I've felt both the excitement and fulfillment that comes with success and the frustration and failure when a job is poorly done — sometimes because of me. High school is an especially scary time: will our students be prepared for their life's journey? I have faced that question twice as two of my teens completed their home school program. I will soon face it a third time with my present high schooler. I expect the question will still receive the respect it deserves when I face it yet again with my two youngest children.

As a pastor's wife, home schooling mother of five, and the part-time manager of a home school department at a Christian bookstore, I usually live a too-busy life. The suggestions contained in this book grow out of a lifestyle that required simplicity in high school planning and record keeping, or they wouldn't get done. (It's still a struggle!) If your moments of relaxation are limited to the last few minutes before the lights go out at night, then I hope this book's straightforward presentation of information will be just what you are looking for!

Since we began our home schooling journey, our reasons for home schooling have grown both in number and eternal significance. Undoubtedly, the greatest blessing and responsibility of home schooling is guiding our children to both a heart and mind engaged faith in Christ. What an incredible opportunity to impact future generations! That knowledge should create a response of awe and wonder in all of our hearts and a reliance on God to be sufficient in our insufficiencies.

The stakes are high; our children's futures deserve our best efforts. Thankfully, God is there for each part of the journey! May He bless us as we walk the road together.

Sincerely,
Diana Johnson
May 1, 2001

OVERVIEW

This Guide Will:

1. Provide information on the benefits of home schooling.
2. Present basic options for home schooling during the high school years.
3. Help you decide which basic home schooling option is best for your teen based on your teen's future goals.
4. Explain how to credit and grade courses, calculate a grade point average, and compile a transcript and other often requested records.
5. Guide you through the process of designing an individualized high school program which will best meet the needs of your teen.
6. Present a course listing which uses a wide variety of textbooks, living books*, and materials available on the home school market today.
7. Provide simple forms for planning an individualized high school program.

This Guide Will Not:

1. Be an exhaustive presentation of all the choices available to you. There are excellent publications already available which have that purpose.
2. Give you a one-size-fits-all home school program. Students have unique abilities, goals, and opportunities. This guide will put the tools in your hands to help you individualize a program for your student.
3. Provide a perfect course listing. All materials have their pros and cons. This guide has benefited from both the curriculum successes and failures of our own home school. However, our situation won't be identical to yours, so add your own good judgment and experience to the ideas presented in this manual.
4. Guarantee a successful home school experience. That depends on you and your teen's diligence and mutual cooperation. I believe home schools will yield some of the brightest stars of our country's future. If your student is one of those stars it will be due to your polishing, not mine!

Living Book: A living or real book is a home school description for almost any book that is not a textbook. Biographies, original documents, historical fiction, novels, etc. are all examples. The premise is that living books are more interesting and therefore are better remembered and more meaningful. Living books can be borrowed from libraries and purchased from bookstores. Living books can either replace or enrich textbooks.

PART ONE

SETTING THE

DIRECTION

THE BENEFITS OF HOME SCHOOLING DURING HIGH SCHOOL

BASIC HOME SCHOOLING BENEFITS

So many reasons to home school exist, and you have probably thought of many of them. Reasons commonly cited are:

Better Academics and Individualized Attention

A tutorial situation is undoubtedly better than a large classroom for customizing education to the strengths and weaknesses of the individual.

Family Unity

Home schooling can slow the pace of life, allowing families more time to enjoy each other and the people God places in their path.

Consistent Religious and Moral Instruction

Many philosophies bombard our teens through school, peers, and the media. Home schooling combats these ceaseless voices with the faith and values of the family.

ADDITIONAL HIGH SCHOOL BENEFITS

Home schooling pursued with faithful diligence provides additional benefits for teens:

Early Work Opportunities

The flexibility of home school scheduling easily accommodates work, volunteer, and apprenticeship opportunities. There are benefits to this early entrance into the work force.

First of all, many teens feel they are in a holding pattern waiting for life to begin. A personalized schooling program, combined with work or volunteer opportunities in the area of career interests, can help provide direction for a teen. This early direction can foster leadership, independence, and a good work ethic. In addition, the adult interaction it provides helps a teen develop into a mature, responsible adult able to communicate in the workplace.

Be wise, however: some teens lack the farsighted vision to continue their education once they feel some financial independence. Don't allow work outside the home if it tempts a teen to drop his high school program. Encourage work as a stepping stone to future goals, not as an academic replacement.

Reduction in Peer Dependence and Increased Parental Influence

Home schooling discourages excessive peer dependence. The varied socialization offered by home schooling clears a teen's thinking and broadens his horizons beyond his peer's opinions and values. This helps place an emphasis on life preparation, rather than on a self-indulgent lifestyle common among teenagers.

With decreased peer dependency more opportunity exists for improved parent-teen relationships. Teens are on the threshold of their future with major decisions awaiting them. Poor choices now often change the entire course of a teen's life and can literally have life and death consequences.

A home educated teen, with more adult influence, has a distinct opportunity to make wiser decisions for his life. Home schooling also gives the parents a little more time to wisely guide their son or daughter. What a wonderful opportunity parents have!

What about socialization?

Anyone can be either positively or negatively socialized. Home schooling provides positive socialization through some of the following ways:

1. The increased interaction with all age groups provides experiences that more closely match and prepare for adult life. A classroom experience restricted to peer interaction cannot accomplish this.

2. Home schooling parents appreciate the opportunity to know their teen's friends and often know each friend's whole family as well. This is a welcome contrast to a teen developing school friendships, for good or ill, without parental awareness.

3. Negative pressures to indulge in bad attitudes, drug use, or promiscuity can be significantly reduced until the teen has the ability to handle these issues maturely.

Any home school parent will assure you that home schooled students have many opportunities to socialize in positive, wholesome ways.

BASIC HOME SCHOOLING OPTIONS

Most home schoolers complete their high school education in one of two ways. They use either correspondence schools or home-designed programs.

CORRESPONDENCE SCHOOLS

If your teen enrolls in a correspondence school, the correspondence school will provide textbooks, course requirements, and oversight of the academic work. This oversight generally includes the mailing in of tests and papers which the correspondence school grades and records. Upon the satisfactory completion of all requirements, a diploma is issued. Some correspondence schools use videos, courses by satellite, or interaction via the Internet. Several of these schools are services of large Christian publishers.

These Christian publishers also sell their complete textbook lines, preschool to twelfth grade, without requiring enrollment in their schools. In addition to textbooks, courses by video (School of Tomorrow and A Beka), satellite (Bob Jones University Press), and software (Alpha Omega) are available for those home schooling independently. Be aware that if you do not choose to enroll in their correspondence schools these publishers will be unable to issue your student a diploma. Purchasing textbooks, without the accompanying accountability of their correspondence services, does not provide the necessary verification of the student's work. In this situation the diploma will come from the parents.

Following are some schools categorized under a few basic descriptions. See Appendix A for address information. If you want more choices than presented here, Cathy Duffy's *Christian Home Educators' Curriculum Manual: Junior/Senior High* or Mary Pride's *The Big Book of Home Learning, Volume One: Getting Started* have much more thorough presentations.

Correspondence Schools

Publishing Company Programs
A Beka* (video option)
Academy of Home Education* (BJU, satellite option available)
Christian Liberty Academy*

Classical Programs
Covenant Home Curriculum*

Worktext (workbook) Programs
Alpha Omega Academy* (Alpha Omega, on-line software option available)
Living Heritage Academy* (School of Tomorrow, video and on-line option available)

On-line Programs
Eagle Christian High School*
Escondido Tutorial Service* (classical emphasis)
SOLA* (Scholar's On-line Academy, classical emphasis)

Secular Accredited Programs
American School
Keystone National High School
Texas Tech University High School

*has a Christian worldview

Should We Use an Accredited Correspondence School?

Accreditation is a voluntary procedure. To avoid the entanglement of unwelcome controls, many Christian correspondence schools choose not to seek accreditation from secular agencies. Some seek oversight from alternative accrediting agencies that offer accountability for Christian schools. Do not assume that a lack of secular accreditation is an indication of poor academic quality.

It is always possible that a college (particularly if it is state funded) could request that your teen have a high school diploma from a secularly accredited school. In addition some colleges, in lieu of an accredited diploma or transcript, have set extra admissions and financial aid criteria for their home school applicants. These may include requiring the GED or SAT II testing.

There has been some encouraging movement toward ending these policies. The 1998 Reauthorization of the Higher Education Act (Pub.L.No.105-244), using language drafted by Home School Legal Defense Association, makes it possible for a home schooler to receive federal financial aid without taking the GED. An accompanying House Report recommends that colleges use the same performance-based assessments for home educated students that are currently in use for applicants from accredited schools, such as ACT and SAT scores, without requiring additional testing. Portfolios were also suggested as a sound assessment tool. See HSLDA's Web site (go to issues, then higher education) for more information.

Despite the law, this issue will not be straightened out overnight. Hopefully, college admission practices will become increasingly equitable over time. In the meantime, appearances can be deceiving. I know of one private college whose catalog states that the high school must be accredited, yet actively recruits home schoolers. We are all still finding our way!

Can We Return to Public High School if Home Schooling Is Not Working for Us?

The answers to this question will vary widely, depending on either your state regulations or your school district's policy. In our area, public schools are very reluctant to credit high school work completed at home, unless it is completed through a state-recognized school. (Accreditation does not automatically mean the school is recognized by the state's education agency.) It has not been unusual for home school students returning to public high school to receive no credit for work completed at home or be required to take an excessive number of tests to validate their work. Check your information carefully before planning a combination home school/public high school experience — and bear in mind that a local policy or the word of a counselor is subject to change, particularly if you have reached an oral agreement only. Your local and state home school support groups are good places to begin collecting the information you need.

Why Do Variations in Home School Regulations Exist?

The federal government often attempts to control education through financial incentives or federal regulations. Despite these efforts, the individual state retains the right to set the standards for their own educational system. Because of this, educational regulations, including those governing home schooling, differ from state to state.

Legal battles fought over home schooling freedoms serve to diminish the differences that exist. When a legal battle in one state results in fewer home schooling restrictions, another state may choose not to fight a battle that was lost elsewhere. Conversely, if one state successfully imposes restrictions on home schoolers, another state may attempt the same. What happens in one state does not go unnoticed in another.

Organizations which work to preserve our home school freedom, such as Home School Legal Defense Association, are very important. Their work across the nation does affect you, even if you never need their services for your personal home school. Consider supporting these organizations with your membership.

Given all the variations that exist, how can you find out the regulations for your state? Manuals, such as this one, can only give you general guidelines. The specifics for compliance to your particular state laws are your responsibility. They should be easily obtainable from local or state home school organizations. HSLDA's Web site can provide basic legal information and help you locate support groups for your state. See Appendix A for address information.

Be aware that laws can always change, and situations that laws do not address are highly changeable when left to the discretion of the current local school board or superintendent. Stay informed!

HOME-DESIGNED HIGH SCHOOL PROGRAMS

The second option, a home-designed program, is what educators call an "eclectic approach." In an eclectic approach to home schooling, an effort is made to find the best possible textbooks, living books,* and materials for each subject. Materials may be chosen from many different publishers.

As a home schooling parent, using this approach means you will choose all of your student's books. Once you've located sources and realize the vast number of choices available, you may feel overwhelmed. That's where this guide can help you.

One purpose of this guide is to offer book suggestions for the home schooling parent. The course listing represents high quality materials available on the home school market. Many products our family has personally used. Others represent materials frequently used by our customers and home schooling friends. Remember, these are suggestions. The best choices are those chosen with your student and situation in mind.

Most choices will represent materials from a Christian worldview. However, I will also be recommending high-quality secular publishers. I will leave it to the parents to sift out the occasional chaff found in these latter books.

This book does not contain an exhaustive list of possible book choices. Rather, my purpose was to present a more selective list for the parent whose time is limited. Should you want a broader range of products to consider, your best sources would be Cathy Duffy's *Christian Home Educators' Curriculum Manual: Junior/Senior High* or Mary Pride's *The Big Book of Home Learning, Volume Three: Junior High to College.* Both authors provide summaries of many popular materials on the home school market today. Sometimes their opinions on a product will differ, so you may find it helpful to read each author's reviews before making a major home school purchase. The opinion of a home school friend who has used the product you are considering can also be an invaluable help.

An Additional Consideration

In addition to all the book and material purchasing decisions involved in designing a high school program there is another important consideration. Because a home-designed program contains no check and balance outside of the parent's supervision, a self-directed program does not result in a diploma unless issued by you. It is certainly appropriate, however, for you to award your teen a diploma in recognition of his graduation from your home-designed program. Before doing so, check with your local or state home school organization to be sure that there are no state regulations prohibiting this practice. Usually there is no problem.

*Living Book: A living or real book is a home school description for almost any book that is not a textbook. Biographies, original sources, historical fiction, novels, etc. are all examples. The premise is that living books are more interesting and therefore are better remembered and more meaningful. Living books can be borrowed from libraries and purchased from bookstores. Living books can either replace or enrich textbooks.

FINAL THOUGHTS

Home schooling your high schooler is a very serious decision. It is time and work intensive for both the parent and the student. It is a call to a higher standard of excellence, not an escape route from problems in a public school experience. It should never provide a cover for truancy. Whether or not a teen receives a quality education and is equipped for the future will rest entirely on the parents' and teen's shoulders.

Knowing the seriousness of this new commitment, if you are ready for the challenge (maybe not ready, but certainly willing to try hard) and excited about your home schooling future (scared may be a better word!), let's forge on ahead.

Why Would We Choose to Use a Home-Designed Program?

First of all, you can choose your teen's books with your student's strengths and weaknesses in mind. A hands-on algebra program may be very helpful to the student struggling in math, while the math genius may be racing ahead into calculus. A teen interested in literature and history can read living books to his heart's content. A history textbook for this student might serve only as a framework for much broader exploration. For another student, the history book may suffice. This flexibility in curriculum choice is hard to achieve in a correspondence school.

Second, you may also determine the pace of the academic work. This individualizing of pace is tremendously helpful to both the remedial student who needs more time and the accelerated student who can move ahead rapidly or desires to slow down and study something in greater depth. In our family's home school, we are spending three years in world history and literature with our current teen because of the high interest level and the depth of study desired. We would not have this much time flexibility if we were using a correspondence school.

A final consideration is cost. Because correspondence schools charge for both materials and the administration of your program (grading, record keeping, etc.) they can sometimes, but not always, be expensive. Planning your own program may cost less because your expense will be limited to your materials.

However, do not choose a home-designed program primarily to save money. It may not happen. Instead, see the money saved by keeping your own records as money now available to use on the material that will best enhance your teen's education. I will gladly pay a high price for a book or program if it will light an academic fire in my teen. Don't sacrifice quality to save money. Your teen's future is too important.

EVALUATING HOME SCHOOLING OPTIONS BASED ON FUTURE GOALS

BASIC PREPARATION

To choose a high school program wisely it is necessary to have some idea of your teen's future career goals.

Junior high is a good time to begin talking to your teen about his interests. Read books about different careers. Talk to people in professions that interest your teen. Visit their businesses. Look into personality or career interest tests that might give some direction. A few helpful products are included in the course listing later in this book.

Once you've determined some areas of possible interest, begin researching to find out the educational path required to meet these potential career goals. The necessary educational path could greatly influence your choice of a home schooling program for high school.

EDUCATIONAL PATHS

My Teen Is Not College Bound

Planning the course work of a teen who is not going to college requires the same care as that of a college bound student, perhaps even more. No school will be following after you to rub off any rough spots you have left in their education. You have to polish the gem all by yourself!

A good course of action for this student would be to investigate career options, apprenticeships, and volunteer opportunities early, since he will be embarking on a career sooner than college bound students. Volunteering to help a carpenter or a plumber, do secretarial work, etc., might open the door to a future career. Be creative and thankful that home schooling provides the flexible hours needed to pursue these opportunities.

Is a totally self-directed program wise in this situation? Perhaps not. It may be helpful if the last phase of a student's education is validated by someone other than mom and dad. For the teen who continues his education beyond high school, his certification or degree from college validates his earlier education. If technical school or college is not in the plan, using a correspondence school may be the best way to insure that the quality of your teen's education is not questioned. A correspondence school can provide enough flexibility to pursue work opportunities while completing a high school education.

Be cautious in making the decision to exclude college preparation from a teen's education. Decisions made today are often reconsidered tomorrow. It would be better to be prepared should college enter the picture at a later date.

Our Daughter Desires to Be a Wife and Mother. Should She Prepare for College?

Raising a God-honoring family is a high calling for any woman. We should be preparing our daughters both spiritually and practically for this role.

Unfortunately, we cannot see into the future and know the situations which may impact our children's lives. Some of our daughters may remain single. Others may find that their husband's earning power is not sufficient for the needs of the family. In addition, through unexpected events, a wife may find herself thrust into the role of breadwinner, either temporarily or on a permanent basis.

Proverbs 31 contains a description of the virtuous woman. It is interesting that her enterprising activities included contributing financially to the needs of her family. There is honor in being prepared for whatever the future may hold. Consider whether college should be included in this preparation.

My Teen Will Attend Vocational/Technical School

The best way to be reassured that the high school program you are planning for your teen is sufficient is to ask questions early. Check into the schools in which your teen is interested. Find out their requirements and then design your high school program to meet them.

My Teen Will Attend Junior/Community College

If your teen's first stop after high school is junior college, either of the home schooling high school options will most likely meet your needs.

Admission standards at a junior or community college are usually not very competitive. Earning modest SAT scores or passing a state-required test (should one exist) and providing a transcript or a GED certificate may be all that is required. Admission requirements change, so get a college catalog, call the office of admissions, and check for current policies.

Once completing junior college many students will transfer to a senior university. To avoid a loss of credits, check with the university to find out what courses they will accept for transfer. If possible, prevent unhappy surprises by securing this information before your student chooses his junior college courses.

ARE THERE BENEFITS TO ATTENDING JUNIOR COLLEGE?

Both of our older children began their college experience by attending junior college. Following is a list of positives and negatives based on their experience.

Positively, Junior College Can Provide:

☐ a transition between home school and an away-from-home college experience. When needed, it provides a little more time for the student to mature, particularly if he completed his high school work at an early age.

☐ a low cost method for exploring career options. It is not unusual for a college freshman to still be unsure of the career direction he desires to pursue. It is also not unusual for a student who has known for years what he wants to do to suddenly begin second guessing. We have experienced both situations. A few exploratory courses may open or close the study area under question. It is much easier for the family or student budget to absorb the cost of these changing plans at the junior college level then at a four year university.

☐ a pardon for negligent home school records. Junior college admissions are usually much simpler than admission to a four year university. With enough credits, your student may be able to transfer to a university on the basis of his junior college transcript alone, giving your record keeping a permanent reprieve!

☐ reasonable student/teacher ratio. This is quite different from the freshman lecture hall course taught by a graduate assistant at the four year university.

☐ excellent teaching. We found teachers at the junior college level tended to expect less background knowledge from the student. This resulted in a careful, sequential teaching style and a teacher available for "dumb questions." For the most part, we found our son's junior college work prepared him well for the competitive university he now attends.

Negatively, Junior College Can:

☐ include students academically disinclined. We found this problem lessened somewhat as the first round of required courses were completed and the least serious students weeded themselves out.

☐ be a social continuation of high school. Local friendships established through years of interaction in public school will continue. If your home school student has a quiet nature, he may find it difficult to find his social niche. Even on-campus Bible fellowships can sometimes be more social than spiritual.

☐ mean missing some university scholarship money available only to incoming freshmen. However, in our situation, a high GPA in junior college earned merit-based scholarship money when our student transferred.

☐ rival universities with their political correctness and anti-Christian thought. Although I have heard this, it has not been our experience — but we live in the Bible belt.

My Teen Will Attend a Four Year College or a University

If your teen hopes to go directly to a four year college or university, plan very carefully and very early. Contact the office of admissions for an admissions packet and catalog *before* you choose a high school program. You will need to choose your home school direction, be it correspondence or home-designed, and all courses with both the college or university's and your state's requirements in mind. Begin to research scholarship opportunities. A lack of careful planning now could lead to great disappointment later. To apply to a four year college or university your teen will most likely need to provide, in addition to the application form:

a transcript. It is much better to know this at the beginning of your teen's high school years so that careful, professional-looking records of an appropriate high school course of study can be maintained. Course titles, grades, credits earned, the date of graduation, and other pertinent information will all need to be included. We will look at transcripts in more detail later.

a list of awards and activities. Colleges want to know that home schoolers can contribute positively to the student life on a busy college campus. Therefore, be sure to include any experiences that highlight well-developed people skills and leadership. Include volunteer or work experience that require high levels of responsibility, initiative, or perseverance. Community service activities such as regular trips to the nursing home, hospital volunteer work, or mission trips all indicate a servant's heart. Athletic, academic, or music awards illustrate the ability to stay with a goal. Include anything that would set your student apart positively from other applicants.

scores from college entrance exams (SAT I or ACT). The SAT I (Scholastic Assessment Test) and ACT (American College Test) are offered at numerous college locations a number of times each year. Calling your local college or visiting their admissions or student services department should provide you with a general information packet for each test. You can also check the test publishers' Web sites at www.collegeboard.org and www.act.org/. (The College Board site has a helpful section for home schoolers.) For a home schooler's perspective, finish out your investigation with a look at Mary Pride's *The Big Book of Home Learning, Volume Three: Junior High-College.*

Since some colleges will not consider a home school transcript an objective assessment of a student's work, great emphasis will be placed on the results of college entrance tests. This puts pressure on the home schooled student to perform at his best on these tests, especially if the student desires to attend a highly competitive college. How can he maximize his performance?

First of all, find out which tests are acceptable to the college your student is interested in attending. If either is acceptable, consider preparing for both. Many test preparation guides are available. Again, Cathy Duffy's *Christian Home Educators' Curriculum Manual: Junior/Senior High* or Mary Pride's *The Big Book of Home Learning, Volume Three: Junior High-College* can provide you with some excellent help in choosing among the many preparation guides available on today's market. In addition, visiting a large bookstore should yield a number of test guides for your consideration.

Secondly, have your student take both the SAT and the ACT tests. Since the tests vary considerably, often a student will score significantly higher on one test over the other. I have often heard it stated that students with strong verbal skills will perform better on the ACT.

Finally, after more study or practice in weak areas, consider retaking the test having the best results. Scores tend to improve with practice. Begin taking the test in the spring of the eleventh grade. Take a final test in the summer or no later than early fall of twelfth grade (or both). Testing after October of twelfth grade may be too late to make college enrollment deadlines, which are usually in late winter or early spring, for the following fall. Students applying under early decision programs will need to complete final testing earlier.

There are two other college board exams that may be of significance.

The PSAT/NMSQT (Preliminary Scholastic Assessment Test/National Merit Scholarship Qualifying Test) is a preliminary test to the SAT I. Although not required, many students take it because it is used for National Merit Scholarship evaluation. High scores on the PSAT can lead to valuable scholarship offers.

The PSAT/NMSQT is offered each October nationally and is normally taken in eleventh grade. Some students take it in tenth grade for practice. (Programs such as the one through Duke University use the PSAT/NMSQT to identify academic talent in seventh grade students. See www.tip.duke.org if interested.) The PSAT is taken at local public or private high schools. Sometimes public schools resist assisting home schoolers, even though the college board has encouraged cooperation. Consider checking with your local home school support group for a home school friendly test location or check www.collegeboard.com for a list of sites in your area. Look into your options months in advance: last minute decisions may make it difficult to find a place that can (or will) accommodate your student.

Another set of tests are the Sat II exams. SAT II's are subject area tests that go beyond the more general testing of the SAT I test. This would most likely be a requirement for a highly selective school or one that questions the objectivity of a home school transcript.

In addition the school *may* require:

course descriptions. Some colleges may desire brief course descriptions to supplement the condensed information appearing on a transcript. They may require a list of textbooks used and books read for each course.

a portfolio of your student's work. This may be necessary when a student's skill needs to be demonstrated for admission; enrollment at an art school would be an obvious example. A highly competitive school or a school unfamiliar with home school students might also require a portfolio.

an essay. This may give the student an opportunity to tell more about himself, hopefully setting him apart from other applicants. Don't plan to remember every unique thing he has done throughout his high school years — keep a record!

a personal interview with the student. A neat respectful student who is confident, articulate, and can look an adult in the eye can excel in the interview process. Practicing an interview at home might be a wise idea. Prepare your student for the questions that may be asked because of your unique educational path. *(Example: How has your home school experience made you a good prospect for our university?)*

   recommendations from teachers, parents, pastors, or employers. Even if optional, a recommendation is a wonderful way to highlight any unique opportunities your teen has had. For example, consider recommendations from an employer, the director of a volunteer organization to which your teen has given time, or a state official in whose campaign your teen has worked. Don't overlook the helpfulness of recommendations from successful college alumni. Think over your teen's activities and request recommendations from people that can highlight your teen's strong points. Set your teen apart positively!

How Do I Find Out about Colleges?

All kinds of ways! Some possibilities are:

- [ ] a campus visit. Many colleges have get-acquainted days which include attending classes and sleeping in the dorm. This is the best way to get an accurate feel for the personality of a school.

- [ ] trusted friends who value the education received at their alma mater.

- [ ] a home school parent with students already in college.

- [ ] your public library's reference section and book stacks.

- [ ] the admissions department, student services, or library of a local junior college. (They may have a wide selection of college catalogs to provide information for those students transferring on to a senior university.)

- [ ] magazines — *Campus Life* and *US News and World Report* special issues. Advertisements in home school magazines will also help you find colleges that are seriously recruiting the home school student.

- [ ] the Internet — you could spend days and days on this information source alone! (www.campuslife.net, www.usnews.com, and www.petersons.com will get you started)

- [ ] college fairs — perhaps your city, like ours, hosts a community-wide college fair. It's a great place to collect college catalogs and find out a college's home school friendliness while remaining anonymous!

How Do I Find Out about Scholarships?

Through old-fashioned hard work and diligence. Begin by checking with the college for any scholarships they offer. A second stop might be the Internet, with www.finaid.com a good starting point. Scholarship information books are also available, such as *The Scholarship Book* by Daniel Cassidy. A stop at your public or junior college library reference section may make purchase of one of these hefty books unnecessary.

During this time, it is highly likely you will receive information about scholarship search services that will help you locate scholarship money for your student; many offers have arrived in our mailbox. Should you decide to use their service, you will probably be paying them well for information you can usually find through your own searching. Check www.finaid.com for information on common scholarship scams.

Once the research is completed, the tedium begins. You and your teen will need to spend many hours filling out forms. Hopefully, the reward will be worth the effort.

Don't despise small scholarships. Many of these go unclaimed each year, overlooked by students searching for larger monetary awards. Encourage your student to consider scholarship research as a part-time job. Should even a small scholarship come his way, the time spent applying for it can convert to an impressive hourly wage.

Finally, have your teen take the PSAT in eleventh grade. If scores are high the scholarships may find you.

My Teen Will Be Entering the Military

The opportunity to enlist in the military immediately after completing high school through home schooling has recently improved significantly.

The most desirable candidates for the armed forces are considered Tier I applicants. In the past, home schooled applicants were not considered Tier I because they were not graduates of an accredited school. This meant it was almost impossible to enlist unless the home school student had completed some college work first.

In the Fall of 1998 a five year pilot program began which automatically placed home schooled students in Tier I. During this time, home schoolers with a home school diploma and a transcript demonstrating completion of high school, who also successfully pass other normal eligibility requirements, may seek enlistment. Should home schoolers recruited during this time period prove an asset to the armed forces, the pilot could lead to permanent recruitment changes for home schoolers. Contact a recruiting office or visit HSLDA's Web site, www.hslda.org. A visit to the issues area will provide some information on home schoolers and the military.

What about the GED?

The General Educational Development test, when passed, certifies that a student has the equivalence of a high school education. Because it is often used as a "second chance" test for students who have dropped out of high school, it is sometimes viewed as attracting a lower caliber of student. Given this unfortunate perception, it may be best to pursue a method other than the GED to validate your student's education.

Also, at this point in time if your teen is interested in enlisting in the military, he will be viewed as a more favorable candidate with a home school transcript and diploma (even if put together by the parent) than he will be with a GED. However, always watch for current information as policies are subject to change.

Having given all the negatives, in some circumstances a GED need not be detrimental. Because the standards at a junior or community college are usually not highly competitive, you may find that a GED offers no impediment to your student's enrollment. After they have proven their ability to successfully complete college level work, students can often transfer to a senior university on the basis of their college work alone. It is up to you and your student to collect the necessary information to make wise decisions concerning the GED. If you can determine that it will have no adverse effect on future educational or career plans, a GED may be an option.

How Do We Preserve Our Freedom to Home School?

Parents entering the home school community now are often surprised at the large amount of freedom they have to control their children's education. Having left their children's education with the professionals in the past, they are amazed to find out they are now "the pros."

It was not always this way. Through the hard work of Home School Legal Defense Association, local and state home school organizations, curriculum suppliers, and early home schoolers (who, at danger to themselves, took a visible stand) the national climate for home schooling has brightened considerably. In every state across our country, parents have the freedom to home school their children.

Unfortunately, the opponents of home schooling are very vocal. This opposition is most threatening when it attempts to curtail our home school freedoms through national or state legislation. When those attempts are successful in one state they encourage other states to increase home school regulation also.

How do we safeguard our hard-won freedoms? Every home schooler can play an active role.

As mentioned earlier, financially support Home School Legal Defense and your state and local home school support groups. They remain our first line of defense against unwelcome intrusions into our home school freedom.

Stay informed of political attacks on home schooling. The above organizations have phone trees, e-mail lists, and publications that will keep you current on potential threats. Subscribe to these services and when action is suggested do your part. HSLDA's Web site, www.hslda.org, maintains a directory of both state and local home school groups.

Most importantly, be conscientious in your home schooling. With great freedom comes great responsibility — and when freedoms are abused they are often lost. It is wonderful to silence critics with success. But far more wonderful is one day hearing, "Well done, thou good and faithful servant," from our gracious God who honored us by entrusting His precious children to us.

Part Two

Mastering the Details

Step-by-Step Decision Making

If you are choosing a home-designed study program for your teen the rest of this guide is for you.

You will probably feel somewhat overwhelmed with the choices before you. Making decisions in a step-by-step process should help. Below is one approach to deciding.

As Your Teen Begins High School Planning:

1. Research home schooling in your state. Know all the regulations as you begin. You will be required to follow them. Your local home school support group or state organization can provide this information.

2. Discuss long-range career goals with your student. Begin seeking out books, resource people, and volunteer or work opportunities that will provide little tastes of career possibilities. This long-range planning ideally should begin in junior high. Plan to continue this investigation throughout high school or until some general career directions become apparent. Don't fret if your junior higher doesn't know what he wants to do later in life. It may be your discernment of your teen's God-given talents and interests that helps determine his general educational path while you and your teen continue exploring career options.

3. Write or e-mail for admissions packets and catalogs now if college is in your plans. Read through the information to find out about all entrance requirements. Know what high school courses and what entrance exams colleges expect incoming freshmen to have taken. Don't find out in twelfth grade that the college your teen is interested in requires three years of foreign language! Read through all admissions information to know exactly what is required. Be aware of any special requirements for home school applicants. Equipping yourself with this information now can provide some peace of mind.

4. Lay out a four year course of study with college and career plans in mind. Decide now what courses your teen will take and when he will take them. Different course guides were consulted to arrive at the general guidelines presented in this book. These guidelines are more rigorous than some because they have college entrance in mind. However, as always, the best guidelines are the high school

requirements of your state and the recommendations of the college your teen wishes to attend. The College Board's book, *The College Board College Handbook*, gives high school course requirements recommended by different colleges. The College Board also makes its own recommendations; these can be found on its Web site www.collegeboard.org.

Consider planning heavier course loads for the first two years of high school to leave more time for "career tasting" through apprenticeship opportunities or part-time jobs in your teen's last two years of high school. This also provides time for visiting colleges and researching scholarship opportunities. However, do guard against a total senior year "coast." This will probably not impress an admissions counselor!

5. Choose the textbooks and resources required to meet your course of study. Our course listing offers many possible choices. Anticipate that this step will unfold over the four high school years.

6. Maintain flexibility. Few ninth graders know what they want to do in life, never to detour from that decision. Adapt your course of study, as necessary, to meet changing career goals. Be patient with your high schooler; some adults are still trying to figure out what career they should be pursuing!

How Do We Help Our Teen Find a Career Direction?

As you and your teen pursue exploratory activities in future career paths, do so with a calm confident spirit. When a teen senses anxiety in the parent to locate "the career destination," the teen also will become anxious. In this rapidly changing technology-driven world, young people are often overwhelmed by the weight of a career decision.

Teens in Christian homes should have a heightened awareness that God created every person with a purpose. God's heart is to guide us to fulfill that purpose. Our responsibility is to be diligent in developing our natural talents and in strengthening our weak areas so that we can bring Him glory. Much time should be spent in prayer thanking God for creating us for a purpose, asking God to show opportunities that will prepare us for that purpose, and listening to God with a still, obedient heart as He speaks to us.

GUIDELINES FOR A COURSE OF STUDY

Planning a high school course of study would be easier if there were clear national guidelines. Thankfully, for the sake of personal freedom, this is not the case. Educational guidelines are developed state by state, with different guidelines for different goals. Private correspondence schools not regulated by the state may offer different options. As home schoolers, our high school course of study needs to meet or exceed the standards that loosely exist if we are going to have credibility with future employees or a college office of admissions.

As mentioned before, your best source for a course of study is always the college your teen is interested in attending. It will have a recommended high school course of study for general college admissions. Additional recommendations for more specialized college majors may also be available. Your state may also have requirements to which you are bound. For example, some states require state history on the high school level; others require this course earlier. Your local or state home school support group can tell you any requirements peculiar to your state.

The following chart contains suggested guidelines which represent a compilation of different public, private, and correspondence school requirements. As you look at the chart, you will notice that it is divided into three career directions: non-college bound, college bound with a liberal arts emphasis, and college bound with a science and math emphasis. Next to each subject are the recommended number of credits to earn, followed by the courses most often taken to provide a well-rounded academic base in this subject area. When the recommended credits have a plus after them (example: English 4.00+) it means it is a good subject area in which to take additional elective credit for that career direction. Consumer math, which appears in parenthesis, is not required but is always a practical course for any career path.

Elective credits can also be profitably used for subjects that are not usually included in a high school plan. Bible, worldview studies, in-depth study in areas of special interest (especially if useful to future career plans), unusual life experiences, etc., are all excellent possibilities for elective credit.

HIGH SCHOOL COURSE AND CREDIT SUGGESTIONS

Non-College Bound		College Bound Liberal Arts		College Bound Science/Math	
Subject	*Credits*	*Subject*	*Credits*	*Subject*	*Credits*
English	**4.00**	**English**	**4.00+**	**English**	**4.00**
English I	1.00	English I	1.00	English I	1.00
English II	1.00	English II	1.00	English II	1.00
English III	1.00	English III	1.00	English III	1.00
English IV	1.00	English IV	1.00	English IV	1.00
Math	**3.00**	**Math**	**3.00-4.00**	**Math**	**4.00+**
Algebra I	1.00	Algebra I	1.00	Algebra I	1.00
Geometry	1.00	Geometry	1.00	Geometry	1.00
(Consumer Math)	1.00	Algebra II	1.00	Algebra II	1.00
		(Consumer Math)	1.00	Pre-Calculus/Other	1.00
Social Studies	**4.00**	**Social Studies**	**4.00+**	**Social Studies**	**4.00**
World Geography	1.00	World Geography	1.00	World Geography	1.00
American History	1.00	American History	1.00	American History	1.00
World History	1.00	World History	1.00	World History	1.00
Government	0.50	Government	0.50	Government	0.50
Economics	0.50	Economics	0.50	Economics	0.50
Science	**2.00**	**Science**	**3.00**	**Science**	**3.00+**
Biology	1.00	Biology	1.00	Biology	1.00
non-lab science	1.00	Physical Science (IntroChem/Physics) or Chemistry	1.00	Chemistry	1.00
				Physics	1.00
		non-lab science	1.00		
Computers	**1.00+**	**Computers**	**1.00+**	**Computers**	**1.00+**
Foreign Lang.	**0.00**	**Foreign Lang.**	**2.00-3.00**	**Foreign Lang.**	**2.00-3.00**
Fine Arts	**1.50-3.00**	**Fine Arts**	**1.50-3.00**	**Fine Arts**	**1.50-3.00**
Speech	0.50	Speech	0.50	Speech	0.50
Drama or Music	1.00	Drama or Music	1.00	Drama or Music	1.00
Health	**0.50**	**Health**	**0.50**	**Health**	**0.50**
Physical Ed.	**1.50**	**Physical Ed.**	**1.50**	**Physical Ed.**	**1.50**
Career/Technology	**1.00+**				
Electives: Include as needed to meet or exceed credit minimums					
Total Credit Minimums	**22.00**		**24.00**		**24.00**

DETERMINING COURSE CREDITS AND GRADES

When we design our high school program, we have an interesting task before us: how to be objective in our crediting and grading while maintaining the flexibility and freedom home education provides. One way is to match our crediting and grading procedures to the materials we will use in each course. A course will usually be based on one of three basic approaches: textbooks, independent reading, or projects. We will look at these three approaches and a logical way to credit and grade each type. Used under the right circumstances, each serves a useful purpose.

TEXTBOOK COURSES

Textbook courses are the easiest for determining credits and grades. They have a well-defined body of knowledge. Their tests and quizzes determine if the material has been mastered.

Crediting Textbook Courses

A student using a textbook that covers a subject in one school year, such as algebra I, would receive one academic credit when the textbook is successfully completed. A student completing a textbook for a one semester course, such as economics, would receive 1/2 credit. Teacher's manuals will sometimes offer scheduling plans for using their books in either a one semester or full year course.

Grading Textbook Courses

Grades can be based on completed reading assignments, discussion of material, scores on quizzes or tests, and papers or projects assigned. Field trips taken and reported on, videos watched and discussed (for example, watching a video on Mount St. Helens while studying geology), or other worthy learning experiences can also be a part of the evaluation process, if desired. You decide what percentage of the final grade to give to each item. One possibility would be:

Course Requirements	Percentage of Grade	Possible Points
Reading assignments	40%	40
Discussion	20%	20
Field trip report	10%	10
Tests	30%	30
Total	100%	100

Grades, even when they appear to be straightforward, are still quite subjective. For example, consider how differently a student would score based on the following situations:

1. The student studies independently and takes quizzes and tests with no specific help from the teacher.
2. The teacher goes over everything to be covered on the test.
3. The textbook is for remedial students.
4. The textbook is college preparatory.

Is the subjectivity described above a problem? Not if used wisely. It is not necessary to make every course equally rigorous academically because all courses are not equally important to your teen's future. Consider setting the difficulty for a course according to the purpose of the course. If a course is college preparatory and represents a future career field, the difficulty of your textbook and amount of work required should be quite challenging. If a course is required but has no significant role in future career plans, use less challenging materials to teach the course. Textbooks vary in difficulty. The courses listed in part three of this book flow generally in an easier to more difficult order.

Advantages to This Method

1. Textbooks are good college preparatory material since a textbook approach will be used in most college classes.
2. Despite the considerations mentioned above, textbooks still present the most objective crediting and grading opportunities.
3. Textbooks follow a carefully designed scope and sequence, providing reassurance that the most important skills and information are covered.
4. Planning a textbook course, particularly with the help of the teacher's manual, can be less time intensive.

Disadvantages to This Method

1. Textbooks don't always have an appealing writing style.
2. Some texts' rapid shotgun blast of facts miss the human drama behind the information they are presenting.
3. Textbooks can be expensive.
4. Textbooks and teacher's manuals will often provide more problems, projects, worksheets, etc., than needed, to provide flexibility in assignments for the classroom teacher. Sometimes the home schooler has a difficult time deciding what to omit.

Textbook Contracts

An easy format for recording your course content and criteria for crediting and grading is a contract. The contract terms can be a joint decision reached by the teacher and the student. At the beginning of the semester or school year the textbooks to be used and content to be covered should be determined. Criteria for earning credits and grades should be settled.

The contract has two pages. The first page records the *planned* goals and the crediting and grading criteria agreed upon by you and your student. Make it as clear and uncomplicated as possible. It can include the projected or actual date when each goal is reached, if desired.

The second page records the *accomplished* goals. These include the final course description, the individual grades earned, and the final credits and cumulative grade. This second contract page will aid you in compiling your transcript and course descriptions (if needed) for college entrance. Filling out the second page as soon as the course is completed will make it easy to record information accurately. This is preferable to working backwards by trying to remember what you did two years ago so you can report it to the inquiring college. Save yourself frustration and keep your records as current as possible — too many of us know this from personal experience!

If you have not kept careful records and your high school program is midstream, you can still correct the situation. Set your course goals and grading criteria now, although it is harder to be objective when you already know your student's performance. Create a course description. Pull out past assignments, quizzes, and tests. Record all your information on page two of the contract form, calculate grades, and sleep better tonight.

The sample contract on the next two pages is for a physical science course using the paces and videos from the School of Tomorrow. Although the first page contains a list of all the pace titles with their completion dates, a few simple statements, such as "Read all twelve paces and watch their videos," and "Complete all written work and lab reports," still contain all the essential information.

The second contract page may look intimidating, but it is really very easy to compile. A course description can be derived by noting section and chapter headings in the book being studied or by referring to the publisher's scope and sequence* or catalog descriptions. This particular sample was constructed using the titles of the different paces and lab report sheets. In addition to the course description, the second page also gives the completed crediting and grading data to be used to calculate the final grade. Plug the percentage grades earned and the activity points you assigned into the chart at the bottom of the page. Do the easy calculations, and you'll have the final grade.

*A scope and sequence is an overview of a textbook. It lists the content contained in each book (the scope) and the order in which this content is presented (the sequence). A full line textbook publisher will often have a scope and sequence booklet where all their textbooks are listed and described.

The course on the sample contract is for a lab science. You will probably notice that the lab work was limited to viewing lab demonstrations on a video and filling in reports. It would have been better to include actual hands-on lab work, but for the "science-phobes" at our house, doing this much marked success! However, change is around the corner. I will need to mend my ways to accommodate one of my younger daughters. Her passion for learning embraces science warmly but is noncommittal about my much loved literature and history.

When you're all done, store your contract in a large three ring binder (three inch works well) with other course contracts. See the following box for ideas on what else to store in this binder.

A Note on Examples

The various examples you will find throughout this book do not represent the academic work of only one student. Therefore, the contract examples will not necessarily match the data on the GPA or the transcript.

In addition, use the samples as an example of an assessment tool in use, not as an example of the best or only way to structure a course's content. The best course is always the one designed for the needs of the individual student.

Where Do I Record Grades and Attendance?

If your state does not have any record keeping requirements, you may find that a course contract along with any other forms suggested in this book, and the student's tests, quizzes, and papers will be all you need to compile accurate records. Don't make it more complicated than necessary.

In some situations you may find a teacher's plan book and record book helpful. *The Homeschooler's High School Journal* by FergNus is a product designed specifically for the home school market. It has sheets for recording attendance, grades, and daily assignments. The daily assignment sheets even include a method for keeping track of timed course work. Other record keeping sheets helpful to the home schooler are included. This product is carried by many home school suppliers.

The three inch binder recommended for storing contracts can be an excellent place to store other remembrance worthy high school information. Good choices for inclusion would be: samples of your student's work, lists of books read, photograph pages full of pictures of special activities and projects (your child posing with his athletic trophy or 4-H project, receiving his Eagle Scout award, etc.), vinyl sleeves containing recital and play programs, state fair ribbons, special achievement or participation certificates, and any other items that would highlight your student's unique personality and achievements. Then, when college admissions time comes, the walk down memory lane will be much easier.

PRELIMINARY COURSE CONTRACT		
NAME: Student	SCHOOL YEAR: 10th, 2000-2001	
COURSE: Physical Science	CREDIT: 1.0	
REQUIREMENTS:		**DATE COMPLETED**
Text: School of Tomorrow paces & videos		
Completion of all twelve paces is required.		
1. Foundations of Physical Science		09/15/2000
2. Composition of Matter		10/06/2000
3. Gas Laws		10/27/2000
4. Chemical Structure of Matter		11/17/2000
5. Metal and Metalloids		12/08/2000
6. Water and Nonmetals		01/12/2001
7. Organic Chemistry		02/02/2001
8. Motion, Gravity, and Energy		02/23/2001
9. Sound		03/16/2001
10. Lights, Optics, and the Electromagnetic Spectrum		04/06/2001
11. Electricity		04/27/2001
12. Modern Physics		05/18/2001
GRADING METHOD		
30 points: video and reading completed		
30 points: completed written work		
20 points: test scores		
20 points: viewed and completed lab reports		
(100 points total)		

COMPLETED COURSE CONTRACT

NAME: Student	SCHOOL YEAR: 10th, 2000-2001
COURSE: Physical Science	CREDIT: 1.0
PARENT'S SIGNATURE:	GRADE: 86% or B

COURSE DESCRIPTION

Text: *Physical Science paces,* School of Tomorrow

<u>Chemistry topics include:</u> definitions and limitations of science, scientific measurement, the composition of matter, gases and gas laws, the chemical structure of matter, metals and metalloids, elements and properties of water, nonmetals, and organic chemistry.

<u>Chemistry lab topics include:</u> electrolysis of water, distillation of water, Charles' Law, double replacement reactions, acid-based titration, reaction of sodium and chloride, reaction of copper and nitric acid, properties of hydrogen, properties of oxygen, properties of water, and dehydration

<u>Physics topics include:</u> laws of motion and gravity, energy, sound, light, optics, the electromagnetic spectrum, electricity, electronics, and nuclear physics

<u>Physics lab topics include:</u> first and second laws of motion, conservation of momentum and the third law of motion, wave motion: reflection, refraction, diffraction, constructive and destructive interference, electrostatics and the Van de Graaff generator, electrochemical cells, nuclear radiation: half-life

Labs were viewed on video and a follow-up lab report was required.

CREDITING AND GRADING DATA

Credits earned for course completion: 1

Percentages Earned

100% — Completed all videos and reading

75% — Completed 3/4 of written work (some math problems were skipped)

87% — Test scores: 100, 92, 82, 89, 76, 93, 93, 82, 85, 88, 78, 87 = 1045

     (1045 divided by 12 tests = 87%)

80% — Viewed and completed lab reports (didn't attempt some application questions)

GRADE

Criteria	% earned (in decimal form)	x	possible points	% of final grade
Videos/Reading	1.00	x	30	30.00
Written Work	0.75	x	30	22.50
Tests	0.87	x	20	17.40
Labs/Reports	0.80	x	20	16.00
			Total %	85.90 or 86%
			Final Grade	86% or B

Should I Use Textbooks in My Home School?

Home schoolers have a great deal of freedom in book selection. That freedom needs to be balanced with the fact that any home schooler entering college will have to function in a textbook world. Your student needs to be comfortable studying from a textbook and taking multiple-choice, true and false, and essay-based tests. If not, he may find himself at a disadvantage competing with students used to this system. Your teen may then be overwhelmed, his grades reflecting his struggle.

We have found it helpful to use textbooks to create college preparatory courses. For at least a few courses during my student's high school years, I use a lecture approach complete with reading and writing assignments, quizzes, and tests. My purpose is to give them as accurate a taste as possible of a college lecture class.

We have also found it helpful to use textbooks in areas where our personal creativity and knowledge are low. Textbooks in math and science are necessary at our home, as I imagine they are in most home schools. We would not be capable of covering all the necessary information without them. However, we tend to use a living book approach to literature and history where our interests take us to greater depths than a textbook would. Even in this situation, however, I find a textbook helpful as a reference or framework to guide our self-discovery.

In addition, textbooks aren't always constricting. They can provide a great sense of relief as you trust them to decide what's most important to cover. They can free you to use your time and creativity in more beneficial areas.

It is common in home schooling circles to see such words as "tedious" and "boring" attached to the mention of textbooks. Broad generalizations are rarely true, and both boring and interesting textbooks exist. Contrary to popular opinion, some students really enjoy the structure of textbooks!

Can I Use the Same Textbooks as the Public Schools?

Probably not. First of all, many textbooks used in public schools are not readily available to home schoolers. Secondly, the adage, "Too many cooks spoil the broth," could be an appropriate caution regarding some textbooks which go through the process of state adoption. The result may not be altogether palatable with many "cooks" recommending adding this to, or deleting that from, the textbook before it is approved. In our age of enforced political correctness and multiculturalism you cannot be sure that only the best materials for study are included in each textbook. Nor can you assume a just measure has been used in deciding how much space to allot to the different topics discussed.

As always, this advice is secondary to your state home school requirements. Presently I am not aware of any state that controls the choice of home school books, but home school laws can always change. It is your responsibility to stay informed.

Do You Recommend Getting All Your Textbooks From the Same Publishing Company?

There are a number of publishing companies that are "home school friendly," making it possible to meet all your textbook needs, preschool through twelfth grade, from one company. This certainly makes home school shopping easy. Is it best for your situation? That depends.

On the positive side, full line publishers work with large staffs, with many knowledgeable people writing and reviewing the curriculum, so material should be very accurate. Carefully constructed scope and sequences mean learning gaps will be avoided. It is comforting to trust some decisions to someone knowledgeable and not feel you must design all your curriculum from scratch — particularly when no home schooler can be equally adept in all subject areas on all grade levels.

In addition, some textbook companies integrate their lessons across subjects. For example, a scientist you read about in your science text may also appear in world history. This provides two opportunities to learn the material and highlights the interconnections that exist between subjects.

There are cautions, however. All companies will have their own educational philosophy. Their worldview will be reflected in this philosophy. Is their position compatible with your family's religious beliefs? Do the texts ever sacrifice scholarship to promote a particular viewpoint?

A publisher's educational philosophy will also determine the basic presentation of material. For example, if its pace moves faster than the norm, can your student handle it? If it moves slower will your student get all you want him to get? Does the publisher emphasize rote recall or critical thinking?

Finally, many textbooks are published with the classroom in mind. This sometimes means there is more material and preparation time than someone teaching several grade levels can handle. Does the company you are considering have a reputation for accommodating the home school market and its differing needs? Do its textbooks and teacher helps reflect that commitment?

In addition to the large textbook companies, many smaller companies have sprung up specifically to service the home school market. Having been originally designed with the home schooler in mind, there are some real gems available.

Be cautious here, too. Remember, anyone (including me!) can self-publish. Therefore, always look for qualifications of the author, accuracy of information, careful work in editing, and reasonable quality in print and graphics. Try to determine the author's educational philosophy. That shouldn't be too hard; we home schoolers tend to be very opinionated!

Full Service Publishers

Before we close our discussion on textbook methodology, it seems appropriate to present some basic information on four of the largest Christian publishers: A Beka Books, Bob Jones University Press, Alpha Omega, and School of Tomorrow. The style of material, educational philosophy, support materials, and availability of material will all be examined briefly.

A Beka Books

A Beka Books publishes textbooks from a conservative Christian perspective with a strong patriotic flavor. Its educational philosophy places a strong emphasis on the rejection of modern educational humanism and a return to Scripture as the source of truth.

Textbooks emphasize the presentation of fact and detail. This emphasis works well with students having excellent memorization skills, but it is less successful for students with learning difficulties. Textbooks are full color quality paperback editions. (Their life can be extended with the addition of rigid plastic covers, such as those put out by the Kapco Company.)

In addition to a full complement of teacher's manuals, tests, and quizzes there are also videotaped classes available for rent. Because A Beka materials are designed primarily for the classroom, you will often find more material than you can use in the home school setting. Rely on the advice of other home school A Beka users as to what materials are necessary and what can be eliminated. Cathy Duffy's and Mary Pride's books may also have helpful advice. A Beka materials are available directly from A Beka Books.

You will notice that A Beka books are absent from the course listings in this book. This does not mean that they are not a good choice for your home school. I am simply limited in my own exposure to them. I have a natural affinity to Bob Jones University Press (see below). Also, A Beka books are not widely available in the home school retail market where I work.

Bob Jones University Press

Bob Jones University Press is another full line conservative Christian textbook publisher. BJUP believes that understanding is vital to the learning of skills and concepts. Practically, this means a child's readiness precedes the presentation of a skill. It also means that understanding precedes memorization. The teacher is considered the key to education; this is not a wind-them-up-and-let-them-go curriculum.

Most of their high school texts are high quality, full color hardbacks, easily passed down to younger students. We have personally used the American and British literature books, enjoying both books immensely. One of my high schoolers actually read through the American Literature book twice. (A feat never accomplished by any other textbook in the history of our home school!)

Support materials include teacher's guides, activity books, and tests. The teacher's guides I used were very helpful in presenting the type of college preparatory courses we were pursuing. BJUP's *Testbuilder Software* provides a convenient testbank for assembling individualized tests.

If you prefer the ultimate in teaching help, BJUP's HomeSat now provides courses through satellite. Along with many elementary grade choices, the most difficult courses to teach on the high school level — math, science, and foreign language — are now available. Through the years BJUP has shown itself sensitive to the home school market. Its annual H.E.L.P. (Home Education Leadership Program) held on the university campus, its quarterly newsletter, *Home School Helper*, its informative Web site, www.bjup.com, and the steadily growing availability of teacher's manuals designed especially for the home school are a few noteworthy examples. BJUP books are widely available through home school catalogs and the newer home school retail market. You may also purchase them directly from the company. A number of BJUP books are included in our course listing.

As a graduate of Bob Jones University, I remain impressed with the commitment to excellence it exhibits in everything it undertakes. (I know, I suffered through some of those high academic standards in my time at the university!) I also appreciate the scholarly, evenhanded presentation of information I have found throughout its textbooks, making them unlikely to offend anyone in the evangelical market.

Alpha Omega

Alpha Omega lifepacs offer a consumable workbook approach to a Christian education. Each set of ten lifepacs contains a full year's work in one subject. They are available in five core subjects: Bible, language arts, math, history and geography, and science. In addition, elective courses in accounting, art, American literature, British literature, consumer math, home economics, Spanish, and Greek are available.

Alpha Omega's educational philosophy stresses both understanding and memorization. This is evidenced by sound study strategies that are an integral part of each lifepac's organization. Main objectives and vocabulary introduce each booklet and section; this provides immediate memory hooks on which to place the forthcoming information. Constant review of main objectives, presented in various questioning formats, aids mastery of the material and extends the learning well beyond simple recall.

The Alpha Omega lifepacs allow the student a great deal of academic independence. Parental involvement is still needed, but not as intensively as with some other materials. If the student reads well and likes well-defined goals and a high measure of independence this type of study may prove very enjoyable for him. He may also enjoy *Switched on Schoolhouse*, a computerized version of the lifepac. Alpha Omega has added attractive enhancements to this program through graphics, video clips, and Web site links.

If your home school has become an impossible juggle of subjects and children, you may find yourself glancing wistfully at a worktext approach. A teacher's manual includes all the parental help needed. Parents will also appreciate the ease in grading the pull-out tests in each lifepac. If *Switched on Schoolhouse* sounds appealing, you may be even more attracted by the grading the program does for you. Alpha Omega products are widely available through home school catalogs and the newer home school retail market. They can also be ordered directly from the company.

School of Tomorrow

School of Tomorrow also offers a workbook approach to learning. Twelve workbooks, or paces, are required to finish each full year course. School of Tomorrow's Christian emphasis includes a conscientious effort to weave character building into each of its courses.

The program is self instructional and does not rely heavily on the teacher. The paces themselves are colorful and attractive. Excellent videos, which greatly enhance the paces, are available for purchase in the high school sciences and maths.

Our experience has been limited to the biology and physical science courses, where we used both the paces and videos. The biology videos drew the attention of the whole family; other work often stopped while we all enjoyed them together. In the physical science course, we found the easy-to-follow, step-by-step presentation of the math concepts very helpful. The videos made a difficult subject accessible and interesting.

The material did seem less in-depth than some other choices, but perhaps the enjoyable format made it seem easier. Students who plan a career in the sciences will want to add hands-on lab work of their own in addition to watching the video demonstrations. See Cathy Duffy's *Christian Home Educators' Curriculum Manual: Junior/Senior High* or Mary Prides's *The Big Book of Home Learning, Volume Three: Junior High to College* for helpful reviews on School of Tomorrow courses. School of Tomorrow materials are available directly from the company.

When Teaching High School Courses Should I Stress Rote Memory or Critical Thinking?

I believe the classical model for education has some valuable insight for us. The classical model advocates progressing from an acquisition and understanding of basic facts to the development of critical thinking skills. Without this underlying factual foundation a student's reasoning can easily end in false conclusions. When the question, "What do you think?" is asked of a student whose head contains little more than his own thoughts, it becomes an opportunity for the student to puff up in self-importance while he spouts ignorance.

The elementary years are the best time to begin the acquisition of basic knowledge and understanding. As knowledge and understanding grow, a student's ability to accurately express, evaluate, and reshuffle that information into useful combinations grows. By the junior high and high school levels the student should be encouraged and actively taught to go beyond "just the facts, ma'am."

Does this mean that the acquisition of information should take a back seat to critical thinking during the high school years? No. The best high school program prepares the student in both areas. A student's body of knowledge should continue to grow along with his ability to analyze it. College professors and courses will have differing personalities. Some will require advanced rote memory skills (an anatomy and physiology course is a grueling example!), and others will require a high level of critical thinking (especially helpful in any of the social sciences where political correctness abounds). A well-rounded high school program emphasizes both skills.

For the Christian a well-rounded knowledge and the ability to reason accurately should mark the beginnings of wisdom. Wisdom will also exhibit itself in a respect for the intellectual achievements of gifted individuals and a healthy humility when we look at ourselves in comparison.

Most importantly, the student will recognize that all true wisdom in all areas of life proceeds from God. The Christian student should be encouraged to study the ideas, struggles, and spiritual victories of laymen and leaders who have faithfully advanced the cause of Christ through the centuries. If our student is to follow their example and actively advance the cause of Christ in today's world, he must have the ability to discern, analyze, and relate information to a Christian worldview. Our student's faith needs to be both heart *and* mind engaged if he is to see his way through the ethical muddle in our world today.

INDEPENDENT READING COURSES

In independent reading courses students pursue a topic through reading, most often using living books.

A living book (sometimes called a real book) is a home school description for almost any book that is not a textbook. Biographies, original documents, historical fiction, novels, etc. are all examples. The premise is that living books are more interesting and therefore are better remembered and more meaningful. They can either replace or enrich textbooks. They can be borrowed from libraries and purchased from bookstores. Home school catalogs promoting living books offer many enticing selections.

In our home school this has been a favorite way to study literature and history. We take our selected historical time period and pursue it reading biographies, historical fiction, documents and literature of the time period, and any other interesting books which cross our path. However, when using living books there are no quizzes or tests to aid in assessment. How do you credit and grade a course like this?

Crediting Independent Reading Courses

Credit can be issued for an independent reading course based on the amount of time spent reading and on any follow-up activities. How do you decide how much time is enough?

In the school system one credit hour is earned in 120 to 150 classroom hours (based on 40-50 minute classes daily for 36 weeks), *plus* time spent in homework.

If your home school is run smoothly with the majority of class time spent "on task," you will undoubtedly get more accomplished in less time. A great deal of time in a school setting is spent on classroom management. Passing out papers, handling discipline problems, and coordinating the efforts of 20-30 students all take up valuable time.

So how much time should be spent? I do not have a definitive answer, but I do know what should be true. First of all, any state requirements, should they exist, must be met or exceeded. If no requirements exist, your decision should be made thoughtfully, with an eye towards preparing your student for a successful future. I do not believe standards should be based on what is minimally allowable, but on what will best help each student achieve his greatest potential. Home schoolers as a group need to strive for excellence if we desire our students to be a positive force in tomorrow's society.

Following is a chart based on different amounts of time representing one credit hour, and an easy weekly way to fulfill the time requirements. The time requirement for one half credit is also given. Class time is based on 60, 45, or 30 minutes, since all break into 15 minute increments. This is much easier to work with than a forty or fifty minute time period. The shaded boxes illustrate the schedule of a ½ credit course stretched out over a full school year. The chart is based on a 36 week school year, but with a little calculation you can adjust it to your particular school year. Take a few minutes to study the chart, and then I will point out a few more things.

DETERMINING COURSE CREDIT				
1 CREDIT		½ CREDIT		
HOURS	WEEKS	HOURS	WEEKS	CLASS SCHEDULE
180	36	90	18	5x weekly for 1 hour
		90	36	5x weekly for 30 min.
144	36	72	18	4x weekly for 1 hour
		72	36	4x weekly for 30 min.
135	36	68	18	5x weekly for 45 min.

On the surface the 180 hours seems very ambitious; however, it represents the total hours spent in a subject which is studied daily for one hour — not a particularly difficult attainment in a home school setting. It should also offer reassurance that when days are occasionally missed you can still produce a quality college preparatory course. Should your student take all his courses by timed credit, which is highly unlikely, he would be spending five to six hours daily on his school work following this recommendation. That is not unreasonable for a rigorous college preparatory program.

The 144 hour goal requires slightly less time than is spent in a 50 minute class meeting daily over the course of a year. The 135 hour recommendation may come the closest to the typical classroom schedule of 45 minute classes meeting daily. Both suggestions are also reasonable goals. The greater efficiency of home schooling should mean more is still accomplished.

It should be pointed out that there are knowledgeable home schoolers who feel that 120 hours (40 minutes daily for 36 weeks) is fine for the motivated home school student. The chart above is not a rejection of that viewpoint, but rather a preference for a system based on 15 minute increments which I find easier to use on a day to day basis.

Once you've decided what your time requirement will be, you will need to determine a way of seeing that the guidelines are met. Three suggestions follow.

1. The most ambitious would be for your student to keep a time record. An example of a time record in process follows this section. Blank forms for photocopying are included in Appendix B. The three record sheets go up to 180 hours. Just stop at the number of hours you have predetermined.

   When combining two subjects into one interdisciplinary approach, such as history and literature, keep two time sheets. Use one sheet for recording the history reading and one for literature. This allows the courses to flow together, but maintains separate records for the transcript. Later, the course description can explain how the two courses intertwined.

2. An easier way to time an independent reading course is to have a reading time established for each day. I utilize this method with my current teen who is an avid reader. Using a timer, he allots one hour reading periods for each of three subjects: history, literature, and a

combined government/economics course. His reading is chosen from a reading list we constructed together at the beginning of the school year. With one eye on our bookcase and another on the catalogs spread before us, we chose books representing different time periods and key events. (When you love a subject, it's a lot like writing a Christmas list!) This reading time, combined with discussions, book reports, or an occasional longer paper, provides both freedom and accountability.

3. What if your child does not enjoy reading and tends to dawdle through reading assignments? In this situation it is helpful to have some idea of his reading speed. This information will help you encourage a timely completion of books, without creating a situation that is too stressful. Reading speed can be derived by timing how long it takes the student to read the first ten pages of the book that he is beginning. This will give you a fairly accurate average time for one page. It's an easy mathematical exercise to then determine how long it should take your student to read the book. Even this is not foolproof; the student can certainly choose to dawdle over the first ten pages! However, over time and several books it should be easier to know when you have set reasonable expectations.

Why Should We Keep Our Standards of Evaluation High?

1. Accurate evaluation gives your teen a realistic picture of how he will perform in college. An overly easy pattern of evaluation can set a student up for an unhappy surprise and potential failure in college.

2. When parents are designing a program for their teen with no external authority to verify the work, they must be extra conscientious about the quality of the work. There will always be home school critics; we don't want the criticism to be justified.

3. Society judges home schooling as a whole by the individual home schoolers they meet. Your teen's success or failure will effect how other home schoolers are perceived.

4. Most importantly, as Christian home schoolers we are not our own; we have been bought with a price. Everything we undertake should be done to the glory of God.

TIME RECORD					
NAME: Amy Jones			SCHOOL YEAR: 10th		COURSE: American History
HOURS	15 min. div.	BOOK OR ACTIVITY	HOURS	15 min. div.	BOOK OR ACTIVITY
1.00	☑☑☑☑	History of Amer. People	31.00	☑☑☑☑	Self-edit summary
2.00	☑☑☑☑	by Paul Johnson	32.00	☑☑☑☑	Edit clean copy w/ Mom
3.00	☑☑☑☑	History of Amer. People	33.00	☑☑☑☑	Summary — final draft
4.00	☑☑☑☑	History of Amer. People	34.00	☑☑☑☑	History of Amer. People
5.00	☑☑☑☑	History of Amer. People	35.00	☑☑☑☑	History of Amer. People
6.00	☑☑☑☑	History of Amer. People	36.00	☑☑☑☑	History of Amer. People
7.00	☑☑☑☑	History of Amer. People	37.00	☑☑☑☑	Democracy in America
8.00	☑☑☑☑	History of Amer. People	38.00	☑☑☑☑	(excerpts) de Tocqueville
9.00	☑☑☑☑	History of Amer. People	39.00	☑☑☑☑	Democracy in America
10.00	☑☑☑☑	History of Amer. People	40.00	☑☑☑☑	Democracy in America
11.00	☑☑☑☑	Federalist Papers	41.00	☑☑☑☑	Democracy in America
12.00	☑☑☑☑	Federalist Papers	42.00	☐☐☐☐	
13.00	☑☑☑☑	Federalist Papers	43.00	☐☐☐☐	
14.00	☑☑☑☑	Federalist Papers	44.00	☐☐☐☐	
15.00	☑☑☑☑	Federalist Papers	45.00	☐☐☐☐	
16.00	☑☑☑☑	Federalist Papers	46.00	☐☐☐☐	
17.00	☑☑☑☑	Book summary — outline	47.00	☐☐☐☐	
18.00	☑☑☑☑	Book summary — first draft	48.00	☐☐☐☐	
19.00	☑☑☑☑	Finish first draft	49.00	☐☐☐☐	
20.00	☑☑☑☑	Self-edit summary	50.00	☐☐☐☐	
21.00	☑☑☑☑	Edit clean copy w/ Mom	51.00	☐☐☐☐	
22.00	☑☑☑☑	Summary — final draft	52.00	☐☐☐☐	
23.00	☑☑☑☑	Anti-federalist Papers	53.00	☐☐☐☐	
24.00	☑☑☑☑	Anti-federalist Papers	54.00	☐☐☐☐	
25.00	☑☑☑☑	Anti-federalist Papers	55.00	☐☐☐☐	
26.00	☑☑☑☑	Anti-federalist Papers	56.00	☐☐☐☐	
27.00	☑☑☑☑	Anti-federalist Papers	57.00	☐☐☐☐	
28.00	☑☑☑☑	Book summary — outline	58.00	☐☐☐☐	
29.00	☑☑☑☑	Book summary — first draft	59.00	☐☐☐☐	
30.00	☑☑☑☑	Finish first draft	60.00	☐☐☐☐	

Grading Independent Reading Courses

It is not that difficult to grade an independent reading course. Below are several suggestions that will provide some objectivity for grading.

1. The amount of time spent reading can determine the course's grade. The more hours, the higher the grade. Again, if the course is important for college or career plans, require more hours.

2. Use narration. This popular home school technique was developed by a nineteenth century educator named Charlotte Mason. Have the student narrate (or tell back) to the parent what he has read. Ask questions that require the student to interact with the material and use higher level thinking skills. *Why does he think this happened? How does this compare to something else? What is his opinion about the information? Does it measure up to God's standards?* Discussions of this nature help develop the ability to formulate thoughts into a logical oral presentation. This may be hard to objectively grade, but you'll certainly be aware of how much your teen is learning. A possible narration grading scale, based on Bloom's Taxonomy of Educational Objectives follows.

GRADE	LEVEL OF SKILL IN NARRATION
90-100 (A)	Can do all of below plus relate own ideas to the information by developing alternative or expanded ideas and defending or criticizing the information for its logic, morality, fallacies, consistencies or inconsistencies, etc.
80-89 (B)	Can do skills below and also analyze the reading for assumptions and points of view, find the main idea, identify persuasive techniques.
70-79 (C)	Understands and can relate the factual content of what he has read. Can also summarize information, make predictions, and judge effects.
60-69 (D)	Doesn't recall material or answer factual questions accurately.
50-59 (F)	Doesn't know what was read or answers questions grudgingly.

3. Write book reports. See page 95 for a possible format.

4. Write summarizations of the most important books read. Each day the student can write a paragraph summarizing the main points of his reading. We found a spiral notebook helpful for this since it kept all the summaries together. When the book is completed, these daily summaries can form the basis for a final book review or analysis. A parent can judge by the content of these summaries whether the student is absorbing the material he is reading. In addition, all the summarization and composition practice will be of great benefit to him when he reaches college. *Format Writing* (section on "The Précis" and "Paragraph Condensation") or

Wordsmith Craftsman (section on writing a summary) are both helpful in teaching these skills. *Format Writing* also gives help in grading these papers objectively.

5. Do follow-up research or opinion papers on interesting topics discovered while reading.

6. Field trips or videos related to the reading can provide high interest additions to your course of study. These can be evaluated, if desired, by discussion or reports. (Or skip the grading and just enjoy them!)

Advantages to This Method

1. Independent reading courses can be a relaxing change of pace from the rigors of math and science courses.

2. They provide a wonderful flexibility which extends to the types of books read, topics studied in greater depth, and the form of evaluation used.

3. Independent reading courses stimulate intellectual growth as they provide an opportunity to begin developing expertise in areas of high interest.

4. If your reading extends to original sources and autobiographies your student experiences the next best thing to being there.

5. The teacher's oversight can also be easier, although books read without oversight will have to be carefully chosen. You may want to discuss controversial books together.

Drawbacks to This Method

Given my enthusiasm for this method, I would be remiss to not mention potential drawbacks. They would include:

1. A reluctant student using it as an opportunity for dawdling or deception. Every student does not love every subject, and you may find little is accomplished when a reluctant reader is working only to fulfill a time requirement. Don't use a method that could place undo temptation in your student's path.

2. A haphazard approach to a subject. Reading selections will need to be chosen carefully. To keep your focus from becoming too narrow, it is helpful to use at least one book or textbook that presents a broad picture of the subject you are studying. In our home this has included using the BJUP *American Literature* book, Clarence Carson's *The Basic History of the United States*, and Steve Wilkin's excellent tape series *America: The First 350 Years* as we meandered our way through American history and literature. This would be too much for the student who dislikes history, but it is my teen's cup of tea.

3. A lack of check and balance. Be sure to use some of the objective evaluations previously discussed and set standards before the course, not after. Then your conscience will be comfortable as you prepare your student's high school transcript.

Independent Reading Contracts

As with textbook approaches, contracts will also work well for independent reading classes. Contracts provide an easy means of keeping track of additional requirements, such as book reports, research papers, videos or movies viewed, and any field trips taken. A list of all books read for a course should also be kept. Books read can be listed on the contract or on a separate sheet if the list is too long. A book list form is included in Appendix B for your use.

Although this may seem like a lot to keep up with, it does not have to be intimidating. The record keeping responsibilities can be shared between student and teacher and completed at different stages of the course.

The preliminary contract is completed before the course begins. It is the result of a joint decision between you and your student.

Time records, if used, and the separate book list is filled out by the student while the course is in progress. We have sometimes used our proposed reading list, highlighting the books actually read and adding any new titles we discovered. This list is used until we are ready to record it in final form.

The completed course contract pulls all the information together into a neat format and includes a course description for future college records. This can be compiled by either the teacher or student. It will then be filed in the binder along with any time records, book lists, and book reports or papers completed.

Following are two sample contracts for reading courses. The first is a possible church history course. Reading is the main focus of the course, but it also includes an oral report and composition requirements.

The second contract is based on an interdisciplinary approach to history and literature which I am using with my present teenager. It began several years ago with world history, and has slowly progressed into American. It's an ambitious program designed for a student who enjoys history and literature.

As already mentioned, consider the contract course a "before and after" situation. The first page describes where you plan to go, along with your crediting and grading criteria. The second page tells where you actually went, what credits and grades were earned, and the final grade derived from that data.

PRELIMINARY COURSE CONTRACT

NAME: Student		SCHOOL YEAR: 10th, 1999-2000

COURSE: Church History	CREDIT: 0.5

REQUIREMENTS:	DATE COMPLETED
1. Read *Sketches from Church History*.	02/00
2. Upon completing each chapter, in a spiral notebook write one paragraph summarizing the most important point or points of the chapter.	02/00
3. Upon completing the book, write a three-five page summarization of the book. Begin with an outline based on your paragraph summaries. Turn in both your outline and paper.	03/00
4. Read one biography on a historical person mentioned in this book.	10/99
5. Write a two page book report on this biography. Follow form provided.	10/99
6. Read the *Didache of the Apostles*.	09/99
7. Read pages 238-273 in *Foxe's Book of Martyrs* on the life and martyrdom of Ridley, Latimer, and Cranmer. Be prepared to relate story and discuss.	12/99
8. Spend three hours reading additional excerpts (your choice) from *Foxe's Book of Martyrs*.	12/99
9. Read *The Westminster Confession of Faith* and *Shorter Catechism*.	04/00
10. Research the history of our denomination. Present a three minute oral report. Must have note cards for oral presentation.	04/00
11. Choose among the following: Augustine's *Confessions*, Luther's *Bondage of the Will*, Calvin's *Golden Booklet*, portions of Calvin's *Institutes*, *The Protestant Reformation: Major Documents*, or other books okayed by me. Read until completing time requirements of 60 hours.	05/00

GRADING METHOD	
50 points: finishing reading assignments	
25 points: book summary & book report	
25 points: oral presentation on history of our denomination	

COMPLETED COURSE CONTRACT

NAME: Student	SCHOOL YEAR: 10th, 1999-2000
COURSE: Church History	CREDIT: 0.5
PARENT'S SIGNATURE:	GRADE: 93%

COURSE DESCRIPTION

This course provides a historical overview of the Christian church. The course includes reading, composition, and oral report requirements.

Sketches From Church History (S. M. Houghton, Banner of Truth) served as the main text.

Additional reading resources included: *Didache of the Apostles, Westminster Confession of Faith* and *Shorter Catechism,* Augustine's *Confessions,* Martin Luther's *Bondage of the Will,* Calvin's *Golden Booklet,* excerpts from *Foxe's Book of Martyrs,* Calvin's *Institutes of the Christian Religion* and *The Protestant Reformation: Major Documents.*

The biography on Martin Luther, *Here I Stand* by Roger Bainton was also read.

The total required reading time for this course was sixty hours.

Composition requirements included a three-five page summary of the main text and a book report on the biography.

In addition to discussions over the readings, a three minute oral report on the history of our denomination was prepared and delivered using note cards.

GRADING AND CREDITING DATA

Credit earned for course completion: 0.5

Percentages earned:

93% — reading assignments: completed 55 hours (55 divided by 60 = 93%)

100% — book summary and book report (awarded 100% of points)

85% — preparation and presentation of oral report (B quality, awarded 85% of points)

GRADE

Criteria	% earned (in decimal form)	x	possible points	% of final grade
Reading	0.93	x	50.00	46.50
Written Work	1.00	x	25.00	25.00
Oral Report	0.85	x	25.00	21.25
			Total	92.75 or 93
			Final Grade	93% (or A)

PRELIMINARY COURSE CONTRACT	
NAME: Student SCHOOL YEAR: 11th, 2000-2001	
COURSE: Interdisciplinary Study CREDIT: 2.00	
REQUIREMENTS:	DATE COMPLETED
(Note: This is an interdisciplinary approach to two courses, which will	
appear on the transcript as:	
Early American History or American History: Colonial-Reconstruction	
English III	
Reading and Composition Time Requirements:	
100% — 360 hours (two hours daily for two semesters)	
89% — 270 hours (90 minutes daily for two semesters)	
79% — 225 hours (75 minutes daily for two semesters)	
Basic Texts and Materials to be completed, with requirements:	
1. *American Literature*, BJUP, through page 335	
one quiz for each subsection, seven in all	04/01
2. *The Basic History of the United States, Volumes 1-3*, by Clarence Carson	05/01
3. *America: The First 350 Years*, tapes by Steve Wilkins	05/01
Additional Reading Requirements:	
Choose titles from master book list, including at least one from each	
list division.	05/01
Composition Requirements:	
A book report for each book read from the book list — one to four pages long	05/01
Five paragraph essays :	
one cause and effect essay (see *Format Writing*)	09/00
one comparison essay (see *Format Writing*)	11/00
One research and one opinion paper — three to five pages each	04/01, 05/01
GRADING METHOD	
50 points: Reading and listening requirements completed	
40 points: Quality of compositions	
10 points: Quizzes	

COMPLETED COURSE CONTRACT

NAME: Student	SCHOOL YEAR: 11th, 2000-2001
COURSE: Interdisciplinary Study	CREDIT: 2.0
PARENT'S SIGNATURE:	GRADE : 97% or A

COURSE DESCRIPTION

This interdisciplinary course covers the courses recorded on the transcript as: Early American History and English III.

Main materials which formed the framework of the course were the first three volumes of *A Basic History of the United States* by Clarence Carson, the tape series, *America: The First 350 Years* by Steve Wilkins, and *American Literature* by Bob Jones University Press.

To The Best of My Ability by James M. McPherson served as a reference on the lives of the presidents.

Additional titles read are listed on the accompanying reading list. These titles included eye witness accounts, biographies, and historical fiction.

Composition requirements included a book report for each book read, a five paragraph comparison of the attitudes of the settlers at Jamestown and Plymouth, a five paragraph cause and effect essay on the role of Presbyterian ministers during the Revolutionary War and the British response (drawn from notes taken while listening to the tape series), a five page opinion paper on the factors leading to the Civil War, and a five page research paper comparing the views of Booker T. Washington and Frederick Douglass.

GRADING AND CREDITING DATA

Credit earned for course completion: 2.00

Percentages earned:

100% — 360 hours of reading time

94% — Composition scores: book reports (90%), 5 paragraph essays (98%), opinion paper (92%), and comparison paper (96%).

(90 + 98 + 92 + 96 divided by 4 = 94%)

90% — Quizzes: 100, 100, 90, 80, 100, 90, 70 (630 divided by 7 = 90%)

GRADE

Criteria	% earned (in decimal form)	x	possible points	% of final grade
Reading/tapes	1.00	x	50.00	50.00
Written Work	0.94	x	40.00	37.60
Quizzes	0.90	x	10.00	9.00
			Total %	96.6 or 97
			Final Grade	97% (or A)

READING LIST	
TITLE	**AUTHOR**
Of Plymouth Plantation	William Bradford
The Mary Rowlandson Story: Captured by Indians	Mary Rowlandson
The Scarlet Letter	Nathaniel Hawthorne
The Young Patriot	Jim Murphy
The Journals of Lewis and Clark	edited by Frank Bergon
Abraham Lincoln's World	Genevieve Foster
Uncle Tom's Cabin	Harriet Beecher Stowe
The Slave Dancer	Paula Fox
The Red Badge of Courage	Stephen Crane
The Killer Angels	Michael Shaara
excerpts from *The Illustrated Confederate Reader*	Rodd Gragg
The Boy's War	Jim Murphy
Call of Duty	Steve Wilkins
My Folks Don't Want Me to Talk about Slavery	edited by Belinda Hurmence
Eneas Africanus	Harry Stillwell Edwards
Narrative of the Life of Frederick Douglass	Frederick Douglass
Up from Slavery	Booker T. Washington

PROJECT COURSES

Some courses are more "hands on" or project oriented. There are numerous examples. Practical life skill courses such as home economics or auto mechanics would fall into this category. Courses designed to teach technical or business skills, such as learning to operate a word processing program, would also be project oriented. Physical education courses based on community activities, such as participating on a swim team or in a church softball league are also activity based.

Some courses can be a mixture of reading, skill development, and application of these skills through community service. For example, a child care section of a home economics course could include reading assignments, CPR and basic first aid training, and volunteering in the church nursery.

How do you evaluate courses of this nature?

Crediting Project Courses

As with an independent reading course, the most accurate way to credit a project based course is by keeping time records. Refer back to *Crediting Independent Reading Courses* (page 39) for the discussion on determining how much time is appropriate.

It is easy to feel overwhelmed with this type of record keeping. Consider ways to simplify the task. A few suggestions follow.

1. If the project course is based on skills you are very familiar with, you may feel that you can estimate the time needed to complete the requirements. This would make the keeping of time records unnecessary. For example, most home schooling mothers would be able to estimate the time needed for various skills in a home economics course.

2. Another option would be to have set blocks of time reserved in your school schedule for working on project courses. It then becomes an easy matter to determine if enough time has been spent to justify the credit you are issuing. If you are following your schedule fairly closely, your student should be spending enough time on task.

3. Lessons outside the home and regular hours of community service are easily estimated without keeping daily time records.

Grading Project Courses

There's nothing complicated here. Working with your student, determine goals and point values. The percentage system used with textbook and independent reading also works well when setting criteria for project courses.

Because project courses are often driven by high student interest, this student motivation may mean little parental involvement is required. However, parental involvement, beginning with the planning stage, can still be helpful. This parent-student interaction can result in a more balanced course. Instead of the student following interests alone, a parent may suggest that the skills learned be more varied. For example, a pre-planned home economics course may mean learning to cook foods in all major food groups, instead of only learning a wide variety of desserts!

In addition, setting balanced goals also prevents any guilt feelings when recording a "doing" course on a transcript. It helps legitimize your student's efforts, in both your eyes and his. It also means you'll be able to produce a course description for the college application process if needed.

Advantages to This Method

1. It provides a method for incorporating the teaching of necessary life skills into your school program.

2. It provides an opportunity to develop skills that may provide lifelong enjoyment.

3. Project courses are a welcome change to the academic side of school.

Drawbacks to This Method

1. The project course is the most difficult to assess accurately. It is difficult to plan a course that is balanced (neither too easy nor too difficult for the student to achieve). Be ready to adjust your goals if necessary.

2. There can be a temptation to credit random life experiences by "stretching" them to fit into a subject's general area. All students, whether in public, private, or home school, have many educational experiences outside of their course work. Public and private school students do not always get academic credit for these experiences. If you give credit, be cautious in doing it. Be sure it is really worthy of crediting and not just a time filler. Time fillers replace true enrichment.

Additional Thoughts

Sometimes a student will develop an all-consuming interest in one area. Maybe it's playing the piano or scribbling stories in a notebook for hours on end. Perhaps it's an insatiable thirst for Jane Austen or Charles Dicken's novels. Maybe it shows itself in a constant upgrading and reconfiguring of the family computer or in a tinkering with anything mechanical.

In areas of such high interest or creativity, tread with care. These types of expression can be highly personal. In a desire to credit and grade accurately we need to be careful to not interfere with the joy of creative expression.

You may decide to leave these areas alone and not formally incorporate them into your school program. If you do choose to credit and grade them, step lightly and keep the criteria simple. Your student is probably spending more time and energy than you would require anyway.

Project Contracts

As with textbook and independent reading courses, the contract can provide a logical assessment tool for a "doing" course. It establishes the activities to be pursued. It records the amount of progress you are expecting in skill development. The standards by which these skills will be evaluated are established in advance. It also moves what could be highly subjective into the realm of objectivity.

A sample contract for a garment construction course follows. (This would be part of a larger home economics course.) Notice that the grading is based on the activities completed and their final quality. It also includes some incentive for character building!

PRELIMINARY COURSE CONTRACT	
NAME: *Student* SCHOOL YEAR: *10th, 1999-2000*	
COURSE: *Garment Construction* CREDIT: *0.5*	
REQUIREMENTS:	DATE COMPLETED
1. Watch video: *Fear of Sewing.*	
2. Demonstrate:	
threading the sewing machine.	
operating the sewing machine safely.	
3. Projects:	
Sew buttons on dress using special video method.	
Alter a pair of slacks.	
4. Watch video: *Pattern Sizing and Alterations.*	
5. Project:	
Choose a pattern and fabric to make a dress.	
Use information from the video to alter pattern properly before	
making dress.	
Follow the pattern directions.	
6. Share your knowledge with your younger sister by:	
teaching her how to sew on buttons.	
helping her make a drawstring bag on the sewing machine safely.	
GRADING METHOD	
50 points: completing all requirements	
25 points: quality of finished products	
25 points: creating a positive experience teaching your sister	

COMPLETED COURSE CONTRACT

NAME: *Student*	SCHOOL YEAR: *10th, 1999-2000*
COURSE: *Garment Construction*	CREDIT: *0.5*
PARENT'S SIGNATURE:	GRADE: *98% or A*

COURSE DESCRIPTION

Requirements of this course included gaining skill in garment making by watching the instructional videos *Fear of Sewing* and *Pattern Sizing and Alterations.*

The student demonstrated her growth in knowledge by:

   threading and operating the sewing machine safely.

   sewing buttons on using the special method presented in the video.

   altering a pair of slacks.

   choosing a pattern and fabric for a dress.

   altering the pattern using tips learned from the video.

   following the pattern directions.

In addition, the student shared her knowledge by teaching a younger child how to:

   sew on buttons using the video method.

   operate the sewing machine safely.

   make a drawstring bag.

GRADING AND CREDITING DATA

Credit earned for course completion: 0.5

Percentages earned:

100% — completed all requirements

 90% — quality of finished work

100% — teaching a younger child and creating a pleasant learning experience

GRADE

Criteria	% earned	x	possible points	% of final grade
	(in decimal form)			
completed requirements	1.00	x	50.00	50.00
quality of work	0.90	x	25.00	22.50
teaching child	1.00	x	25.00	25.00
			Total %	97.5 or 98
			Final Grade	98 (or A)

GENERAL THOUGHTS ON CREDITING AND GRADING

On Letter Vs. Numerical Grades

One of the decisions you will need to make when designing your high school program is whether to use letter or numerical (percentage) grades.

Percentage grades are the most objective and are easy to calculate on a test or quiz. If you set your criteria for reading or project courses on a point basis, you can also use numerical grades in these more subjective areas. All the contract examples given previously will result in a numerical, or percentage-based grade.

If for some reason you decide to change to letter grades, it is a simple matter to convert. It is not as easy to work backward from a less precise letter grade to a precise numerical grade. If you choose to use letter grades you will also have to decide whether to use just the letters (A, B, C, D) or gradate them into smaller units (A+, A, A-).

Either letter or numerical grades can be used on a transcript. Numerical grades are straightforward and don't require an admissions counselor to refer to constantly changing grading scales from one transcript to another. However, you may want to use the grading system most common in your area.

Both letter and numerical grades can be converted into a grade point average. Whatever your decision, the chart below will help you. It is a conversion chart for changing numerical grades into letter grades and vice versa, along with GPA information. Please note that different grading scales exist; this is just one possibility.

Letter Grades With Number Grade Equivalent and Grade Points									
A			B			C			D/F
A+	A	A-	B+	B	B-	C+	C	C-	Failing
98-100	94-97	90-93	88-89	84-87	80-83	78-79	74-77	70-73	0-69
4.0			3.0			2.0			0.0

On Grading Nonacademic Classes

Should all courses receive a grade, or can physical education and other nonacademic courses receive a pass/fail designation?

First of all, it is possible to grade these courses. Courses of this nature can be set up on a contract resulting in a numerical grade. Just keep your grading criteria straightforward and simple. In our area, all courses are graded (and included in the grade point average).

Unfortunately a pass/fail designation can appear as a means of hiding substandard work. With the national debate on the failures of our educational system continuing, there is an ongoing movement towards a greater accountability. This trend in itself could mark the eventual demise of a pass/fail option. For this reason, I would recommend grading all courses.

On Record Keeping

It is easy to become overwhelmed with the bookkeeping aspects of home schooling. To preserve your sanity, remember that any methodology you choose for creating and recording credits or grades needs to serve your needs, not enslave you. An overly elaborate record keeping or grading system can be very time consuming. And time spent in record keeping is time not spent in teaching, interacting with your student, or in having a life outside of home schooling. If you are teaching more than one student (which most of us are) complicated crediting and grading systems may not be completed, making you feel like a failure.

Particularly freeing for me was observing the grading plans of my two oldest children's college professors. A significant variation existed in the way a student's course work was assessed. Some professors based their final grade on numerous intermediate grades, some on only a few. It left me with a comfortable feeling that as long as the student's work is being fairly evaluated, simpler methods are fine. Just be sure to set some expectations, however simple, in advance. Expectations that change too readily without good reason do not prepare a student for the inflexible guidelines that will exist in many college level courses.

It would be nice to avoid record keeping altogether. However, it does serve a second function just as important as preparing credible college records. It also teaches your student how to objectively evaluate his work and recognize when he has done exceptional, average, or inferior work. The student's ability to honestly assess his performance can help him form a healthy appreciation for his strengths and an understanding of his weaknesses. This knowledge can help him make realistic decisions concerning college majors and future career directions.

To ease the burden of record keeping, share it with your student. After all, since the records are for his future benefit, he needs to take some ownership of the process. Working from goals you have created together, the task of any daily record keeping can be the task of the student with the teacher providing oversight as needed.

Should you find my crediting and grading suggestions too complicated or my forms too unwieldy for your situation, simplify them to meet your needs. I have rarely found that the forms designed by others satisfy the needs of my family and home school. Use my ideas and forms as a springboard to create the right guidelines for your situation.

CALCULATING A GRADE POINT AVERAGE

A grade point average or GPA is often included on a transcript. A GPA is an average of all the grades earned during high school converted (most often) to a four point scale.

Calculating a GPA can be a complicated process. One complication is "weighting" courses. This involves giving bonus points for more difficult work, such as honors or advanced placement courses. Weighting can also involve lowering the points for remedial classes.

Should a home school parent ever weight a course? To avoid questions about parental subjectivity, you might consider weighting a course only if the course work is verifiable by some outside authority. Early enrollment courses at the junior or community college or advanced placement test results would fit this criteria.

There is no national standard for how much additional weight to give difficult courses. One possibility is raising the grade by ten points when using a numerical grade or by one letter grade when using letter grades. This is easy with percentage grades — each course grade could be raised ten points. This is harder with letter grades: how do you go up from an A?

A better option may be to raise the course's grade point by one point. In our example table, English 1301 and 1302 were taken for dual credit (credit for both high school and college) in twelfth grade. A score of 95 (or A) was earned in English 1301, and an 89 (or B) in English 1302. When assigning a GPA, English 1301 receives five points. English 1302 receives four. Each course has gained one extra grade point for being a college level course. (See the following sample worksheets.)

If you weight a grade, give the college admissions counselor some transcript clue as to why these courses received an extra grade point. Consider asterisking these courses on the transcript, referring the admissions counselor to a notation stating that college level (or advanced placement) courses were awarded one extra grade point.

When you study the GPA worksheets you will notice that the elective Bible courses are followed by double asterisks. These courses were half-credit courses (only one half hour was spent daily) taken over the course of the year. Grades for the year were compiled and included only for the second semester. Recording the grade twice would inaccurately record it as a full credit course.

Notice also that the worksheet compiles grade points by the semester. This makes it easier to calculate the GPA by semester. High school transcripts sent out in late winter for fall college enrollment will then have information current through the first semester of twelfth grade.

Notice that all courses, even nonacademic, were included in the GPA. Unless you have accurate information to the contrary, I would recommend including all credited courses. However, it is possible that things are handled differently in different parts of the country. For a second opinion a friendly high school guidance counselor can provide accurate information.

The following boxes and worksheets will walk you through converting the sample transcripts (pages 67-68) into grade point averages. A blank worksheet is included in Appendix B to help you in your GPA calculations. It should *not* be turned in as part of your transcript.

Computing a GPA Based on Numerical Grades

1. Record each course's numerical grade by semester.

2. Convert the numerical grades to a four point scale. Add one point for any advanced placement or college level courses. See asterisks in chart.

3. Record the number of semesters spent in each class.

4. Total the number of grade points and the semesters spent in class each year. (Example: 29 and 29 grade points and 16 semesters of class).

5. Add both semester's grade points together and divide by the total number of semesters spent in class that year. This is the grade point average for the school year (Example: 29 + 29 = 58, divide this by 16 to get 3.63).

6. Repeat this process for each year of high school.

7. Add together the grade point averages from all four years of high school. (Example: 3.63 + 3.65 + 3.38 + 3.67 = 14.33).

8. Divide this grade point sum by four (Example: 14.33 divided by 4 = 3.58). The cumulative grade point average is 3.58. Record this on the transcript.

COMPUTING A GPA FROM NUMERICAL (PERCENTAGE) GRADES

NINTH GRADE					TENTH GRADE				
COURSE	1st semester grade/points		2nd semester grade/points		# of semesters	COURSE	1st semester grade/points		2nd semester grade/points		# of semesters
English I	95	4	93	4	2	English II	98	4	92	4	2
Algebra I	86	3	86	3	2	Geometry	88	3	84	3	2
World Geography	98	4	93	4	2	American History	97	4	91	4	2
Physical Science	81	3	76	2	2	Biology	85	3	86	3	2
Word Processing	94	4	92	4	2	Latin II	84	3	90	4	2
Latin I	86	3	92	4	2	Piano	90	4	90	4	2
Piano	90	4	90	4	2	Church History**			87	3	1
Bible Survey**			97	4	1	Home Economics	93	4	97	4	2
PE	95	4			1	Physical Education	95	4	93	4	2
Total grade points by semester	29		29		16	Total grade points by semester	29		33		17
Total grade points and semesters	58				16	Total grade points and semesters	62				17
Total grade points for year divided by total semesters of class = GPA			3.63			Total grade points for year divided by total semesters of class = GPA			3.65		

ELEVENTH GRADE					TWELFTH GRADE				
COURSE	1st semester grade/points		2nd semester grade/points		# of semesters	COURSE	1st semester grade/points		2nd semester grade/points		# of semesters
English III	91	4	89	3	2	English 1301 & 1302	95	5*	89	4*	2
Creative Writing			96	4	1	Consumer Math	95	4	96	4	2
Algebra II	79	2	77	2	2	Government	87	3			1
World History	98	4	96	4	2	Economics			85	3	1
Latin III	86	3	88	3	2	Geology	86	3			1
Piano	90	4	90	4	2	Astronomy	84	3			1
Speech	86	3			1	Piano	90	4	90	4	2
Bible Doctrines**			96	4	1	Worldview Study**			86	3	1
						Health	90	4			1
Total grade points by semester	20		24		13	Total grade points by semester	26		18		12
Total grade points and semesters	44				13	Total grade points and semesters	44				12
Total grade points for year divided by total semesters of class = GPA			3.38			Total grade points for year divided by total semesters of class = GPA			3.67		

Add four yearly grade points together (3.63 + 3.65 + 3.38 + 3.67 = 14.33)
Divide total grade points by four to get final grade point average (14.33 divided by four = 3.58)
FINAL GRADE POINT AVERAGE = 3.58

Is It Necessary to Include a GPA on the Transcript?

The GPA calculation is an important one. Expect to see the GPA requested on the college and scholarship applications your student fills out.

However, some high schools report student GPA's as a percentage average (86%, 95%, etc.) instead of converting it to a four point system. If this is acceptable with the colleges or scholarships being considered, it will save you and your student one small step.

Computing a GPA Based on Letter Grades

1. Record each course's letter grade by semester.

2. Convert the letter grades to a four point scale. Add one point for any advanced placement or college level courses. See asterisks in chart.

3. Record the number of semesters spent in each class.

4. Total the number of grade points and the semesters spent in class each year. (Example: 29 and 29 grade points and 16 semesters of class).

5. Add both semester's grade points together and divide by the total number of semesters spent in class that year. This is the grade point average for the school year (Example: 29 + 29 = 58, divide this by 16 to get 3.63).

6. Repeat this process for each year of high school.

7. Add together the grade point averages from all four years of high school. (Example: 3.63 + 3.65 + 3.38 + 3.67 = 14.33).

8. Divide this grade point sum by four (Example: 14.33 divided by 4 = 3.58). The cumulative grade point average is 3.58. Record this on the transcript.

COMPUTING A GPA FROM LETTER GRADES

NINTH GRADE

COURSE	1st semester grade/points		2nd semester grade/points		# of semesters
English I	A	4	A	4	2
Algebra I	B	3	B	3	2
World Geography	A	4	A	4	2
Physical Science	B	3	C	2	2
Word Processing	A	4	A	4	2
Latin I	B	3	A	4	2
Piano	A	4	A	4	2
Bible Survey**			A	4	1
PE	A	4			1
Total grade points by semester	29		29		16
Total grade points and semesters	58				16
Total grade points for year divided by total semesters of class = GPA	3.63				

TENTH GRADE

COURSE	1st semester grade/points		2nd semester grade/points		# of semesters
English II	A	4	A	4	2
Geometry	B	3	B	3	2
American History	A	4	A	4	2
Biology	B	3	B	3	2
Latin II	B	3	A	4	2
Piano	A	4	A	4	2
Church History**			B	3	1
Home Economics	A	4	A	4	2
Physical Education	A	4	A	4	2
Total grade points by semester	29		33		17
Total grade points and semesters	62				17
Total grade points for year divided by total semesters of class = GPA	3.65				

ELEVENTH GRADE

COURSE	1st semester grade/points		2nd semester grade/points		# of semesters
English III	A	4	B	3	2
Creative Writing			A	4	1
Algebra II	C	2	C	2	2
World History	A	4	A	4	2
Latin III	B	3	B	3	2
Piano	A	4	A	4	2
Speech	B	3			1
Bible Doctrines**			A	4	1
Total grade points by semester	20		24		13
Total grade points and semesters	44				13
Total grade points for year divided by total semesters of class = GPA	3.38				

TWELFTH GRADE

COURSE	1st semester grade/points		2nd semester grade/points		# of semesters
English 1301 & 1302	A	5*	B	4*	2
Consumer Math	A	4	A	4	2
Government	B	3			1
Economics			B	3	1
Geology	B	3			1
Astronomy	B	3			1
Piano	A	4	A	4	2
Worldview Study**			B	3	1
Health	A	4			1
Total grade points by semester	26		18		12
Total grade points and semesters	44				12
Total grade points for year divided by total semesters of class = GPA	3.67				

Add four yearly grade points together (3.63 + 3.65 + 3.38 + 3.67 = 14.33)

Divide total grade points by four to get final grade point average (14.33 divided by four = 3.58)

FINAL GRADE POINT AVERAGE = 3.58

Should Our College Admissions Paperwork Identify Our Student as a Home Schooler?

In years past, when home schooling was largely unknown, some home schooling families chose to send in college applications which identified their home school as a private school (a legitimate legal definition of home schooling in many states). With the growing awareness of home schooling as a national movement, the necessity of such an action seems to be disappearing.

If your teen is interested in a small private college it is probably not a problem to identify your student as a home schooler. Admissions will be handled on a smaller, more individualized basis. Christian colleges should not be a problem for the home schooler. A large portion of the home school community has a Christian worldview. Christian colleges and universities are very aware of this and often actively recruit home schoolers.

If problems arise it is more likely to happen with large universities. However, with the rapid rise in the number of home schoolers it is unlikely that home schoolers are a new concept to them. Many schools now have admission policies specifically for home schoolers. It is important to know what these policies are and abide by them.

Because of the large number of applicants, the selection of students may be very impersonal out of necessity. Should a computer (or a person with a checklist) do the initial processing, an application that is not standard may be set aside. In this situation you will want to follow all admissions requirements very carefully and not create an unusual situation that will delay or prevent your application from being processed. In addition, you do not want to create extra work for a busy admissions counselor. Expecting special concessions as a home schooler may have an arrogant appearance that will not help a student's application process.

Some colleges have very selective admission standards where all accepted applicants will be high achievers. The high achievement of a home schooler will reflect the norm and may not give him an edge over other applicants. Here it is also important to play by the rules.

In trying to determine a university's attitude towards home schoolers your best advice will come from other home schoolers who have sought admission at the same university. The admissions packet and catalog may also offer clues as to the school's attitude towards home schooling. A visit to the HSLDA Web site (search by college admissions policies) or the home school organization in the state where the college is located may provide valuable information about a school's policies and attitude towards home schoolers.

In the past five to ten years, the first large wave of home schoolers began arriving at many colleges and universities. Hopefully, their success will result in a growing recruitment of home school students by schools across our nation.

Compiling a Transcript

A transcript is a compilation of all the courses your student has taken each year along with the credits and grades he has earned. If you have pursued a home-designed high school program it is up to you to use the records you have been keeping to compile the transcript.

A transcript usually includes:

1. biographical information on the student.
2. a date of graduation.
3. the number of credits earned.
4. the student's grade point average.
5. courses listed individually, grouped by academic year.
6. grades for each course. Include grades for each semester and a final grade. Do early or mid-January calculations on grades earned thus far to arrive at first semester totals. Use the grades for the rest of the year for second semester calculations.
A second option is to report yearly grades *if* you know these are acceptable to the college your student is considering.
7. transcript grades recorded as numbers (78, 89, 95, etc.) or letters (A, B, C, etc.). Use the system most prevalent in your area.
8. the grading scale that was used, if using letter grades.
9. a school seal. Some colleges require all official transcripts to be embossed with a seal bearing the school's name. You can order a seal (attached to an embossing tool) from many office supply stores. They will customize the seal with your school's name and any other design you would like.
10. the date the transcript was issued. Most transcripts will be sent out before the student has completed his senior year (leave the last semester and final grades for twelfth grade blank). Including an issue date helps the college admissions department keep up with which transcript is the newest and most complete, should you send a second, final transcript. For an incomplete transcript, the graduation date can be called a projected graduation date, if desired.

Transcripts can be constructed in different ways. The key is including the information above in a neat, professional, and understandable format. Two possible transcripts follow, one based on percentage and one on letter grades. The second is complete through first semester twelfth grade. Blank transcript forms are included in Appendix B. Cathy Duffy's *Christian Home Educators' Curriculum Manual: Junior/Senior High* has another possibility.

Note: You will notice we had the father sign the administrative signature. This could read parent's signature if the school welcomes home school applicants.

Do High Grades Make a Transcript Impressive?

It is not always the highest grades that make a transcript impressive. Two reasons are:

1. Grades are subjective and may or may not be an accurate reflection of a student's ability. High grades should be backed up by high scores on college entrance tests.

2. Easy classes with straight "A's" may not be as impressive as difficult courses with slightly lower grades.

All This Talk of Credits, Grades, Transcripts, and Grade Point Averages Makes Me Panic; Can I Do All This Right?

Try to relax! If there has been one recurrent word in discussing these topics, it has been the word "subjective." No national standard exists for any of these concerns, so there is not one right way to do things. Particularly frustrating is recommending guidelines for GPA's; there are tremendous variations in how they are determined.

However, having said that, some general principles do apply. Fairly and accurately portray your student's high school work. The college will be expecting your teen to perform for them at the same academic level shown on his high school transcript. ACT or SAT scores should also reflect the same student ability. If high school grades are far higher than SAT scores, the quality of your high school program will surely be placed in question.

Present all information in a clear, consistent, and understandable format. Computers do a great job of accomplishing this!

How Important is a Diploma?

The diploma is given as a recognition of academic achievement, not as proof of that achievement. A transcript of courses taken and grades earned, and SAT or ACT scores that back up those grades, are the real proof that a high school program has merit.

Unless there are state laws prohibiting it, by all means give your hard-working graduate a diploma to show that you honor him and his achievement. It may decorate his office wall someday! A professional quality, ready-to-fill-in diploma is available through Home School Legal Defense Association and some state home school organizations.

ACADEMIC TRANSCRIPT RECORD

Name: Student

ADDRESS: 521 E. School Ave.
Tyler, TX 75701

Date of Birth: 4/17/81 **Sex:** Female

Social Security Number: 000 00 0000

Administrator's Signature: *Mr. Administrator*

School: Covenant Christian School

Address: PO. Box 123 Tyler, TX

Credits Earned: 29.0   **GPA:** 3.58

Date of Graduation: 5/26/99

Date Transcript Issued: 06/04/99

Date of College Entry: Fall 1999

NINTH GRADE

COURSE	1ST SEM	2ND SEM	FINAL GRADE	CREDIT
English I	95	93	94	1.00
Algebra I	86	86	86	1.00
World Geography	98	93	96	1.00
Physical Science	81	76	79	1.00
Word Processing	94	92	93	1.00
Latin I	86	92	89	1.00
Piano I	90	90	90	1.00
Bible Survey	97	97	97	0.50
Physical Education	95	95	95	0.50

YEAR: 95/96

9TH GRADE GPA: 3.63   **9TH GRADE CREDITS: 8.00**

TENTH GRADE

COURSE	1ST SEM	2ND SEM	FINAL GRADE	CREDIT
English II	98	92	95	1.00
Geometry	88	84	86	1.00
American History	97	91	94	1.00
Biology	85	86	86	1.00
Latin II	84	90	87	1.00
Piano II	90	90	90	1.00
Church History	87	87	87	0.50
Home Economics	93	97	95	1.00
Physical Education	95	93	94	1.00

YEAR: 96/97

10TH GRADE GPA: 3.65   **10TH GRADE CREDITS: 8.50**

ELEVENTH GRADE

COURSE	1ST SEM	2ND SEM	FINAL GRADE	CREDIT
English III	91	89	90	1.00
Creative Writing	96	96	96	0.50
Algebra II	79	77	78	1.00
World History	98	96	97	1.00
Latin III	86	88	87	1.00
Piano III	90	90	90	1.00
Speech	86	86	86	0.50
Bible Doctrines	96	96	96	0.50

YEAR: 97/98

11TH GRADE GPA: 3.38   **11TH GRADE CREDITS: 6.50**

TWELFTH GRADE

COURSE	1ST SEM	2ND SEM	FINAL GRADE	CREDIT
English 1301 & 1302 *college dual credit	95	89	90	1.00
Consumer Math	95	96	96	1.00
Government	87		87	0.50
Economics		85	85	0.50
Geology	86	86	86	0.50
Astronomy	84	84	84	0.50
Piano IV	90	90	90	1.00
Worldview Studies		86	86	0.50
Health	90	90	90	0.50

YEAR: 98/99

12TH GRADE GPA: 3.67   **12TH GRADE CREDITS: 6.00**

One credit hour represents between 135-180 hours of work.

*College course work received one extra grade point.

ACADEMIC TRANSCRIPT RECORD

Name:	Student		School:	Covenant Christian School
ADDRESS:	521 E. School Ave.		Address:	P.O. Box 123 Tyler, TX
	Tyler, TX 75701		Credits Earned: 26.5	GPA: 3.58
Date of Birth: 4/17/81	Sex: Female		Projected Graduation:	5/26/99
Social Security Number: 000 00 0000			Date Transcript Issued:	01/15/99
Administrator's Signature: Mr. Administrator			Date of College Entry:	Fall 1999

NINTH GRADE — YEAR: 95/96

COURSE	1ST SEM	2ND SEM	FINAL GRADE	CREDIT
English I	A	A	A	1.00
Algebra I	B	B	B	1.00
World Geography	A	A	A	1.00
Physical Science	B	C	C	1.00
Word Processing	A	A	A	1.00
Latin I	B	A	B	1.00
Piano I	A	A	A	1.00
Bible Survey		A	A	0.50
Physical Education	A		A	0.50

9TH GRADE GPA: 3.63   9TH GRADE CREDITS: 8.00

ELEVENTH GRADE — YEAR: 97/98

COURSE	1ST SEM	2ND SEM	FINAL GRADE	CREDIT
English III	A	B	A	1.00
Creative Writing		A	A	0.50
Algebra II	C	C	C	1.00
World History	A	A	A	1.00
Latin III	B	B	B	1.00
Piano III	A	A	A	1.00
Speech	B		B	0.50
Bible Doctrines		A	A	0.50

11TH GRADE GPA: 3.38   11TH GRADE CREDITS: 6.50

TENTH GRADE — YEAR 96/97

COURSE	1ST SEM	2ND SEM	FINAL GRADE	CREDIT
English II	A	A	A	1.00
Geometry	B	B	B	1.00
American History	A	A	A	1.00
Biology	B	B	B	1.00
Latin II	B	A	B	1.00
Piano II	A	A	A	1.00
Church History		B	B	0.50
Home Economics	A	A	A	1.00
Physical Education	A	A	A	1.00

10TH GRADE GPA: 3.65   10TH GRADE CREDITS: 8.50

TWELFTH GRADE — YEAR: 98/99

COURSE	1ST SEM	2ND SEM	FINAL GRADE	CREDIT
English 1301 & 1302 *college dual credit	A			0.50
Consumer Math	A			0.50
Government	B			0.50
Economics				0.50
Geology	B			0.50
Astronomy	B			0.50
Piano IV	A			0.50
Worldview Studies				
Health	A			0.50

1ST SEMESTER GPA: 3.71   12TH GRADE CREDITS: 3.50

Grading Scale: A: 90-100 B: 80-89 C: 70-79 D: 60-69 F: 0-59

1 Credit hour =135-180 hours   *College courses received 1 extra grade point

Titling Alpha Omega Courses on a Transcript

If you are interested in using the Alpha Omega lifepacs, you will soon notice the generic titles for the courses. How do you record *History and Geography: 10th Grade* or *Math: 9th Grade* on a transcript?

Fortunately, Alpha Omega's scope and sequence provides the information needed to title most classes with traditional high school names. These titles will work with either the lifepacs or the *Switched on Schoolhouse* computerized version.

The following titles reflect the content of the various lifepacs.

Bible*

9th: New Testament Survey

10th: Old Testament Survey

11th: Major Biblical Themes I

12th: Major Biblical Themes II

Language Arts	*Math*
9th: English I	9th: Algebra I
10th: English II	10th: Geometry
11th: English III	11th: Algebra II
12th: English IV	12th: Advanced Math

History	*Science*
9th: Social Studies**	9th: Physical Science***
10th: World History	10th: Biology
11th: U.S. History	11th: Chemistry
12th: Government/Economics	12th: Physics

*Bible courses will most likely be viewed as electives and not academic core courses. Therefore their transcript titles are not of great concern.

**9th grade history and geography is a general study of civics, careers, and world geography. This is the hardest course to give a traditional high school title. Consider calling it Social Studies or supplement with additional geography reading and activities and call it World Geography. If you want a lifepac course that is only geography use their half year *Lifepac Select Geography* and supplement with map making, report writing, etc. to make a full year course.

***This is a two year study, with Alpha Omega titling 8th grade *Physical Science I* and 9th grade *Physical Science II*. In reviewing the scope and sequence, however, it appears that 8th grade primarily covers physical science while 9th grade gives a general science overview.

ADDITIONAL RECORDS

The last details to look at are additional records that sometimes accompany the transcript. We have already taken a look at these on pages 14-16. However, let's take a moment to look again at a few that may be unique to home schoolers.

Additional records sometimes required or recommended for home schoolers include:

1. *a record of special awards and activities.* The application will include space for awards and activities, but you may not feel it adequate to showcase your student's unique opportunities. If that is the case, then enclose a separate activities and awards list. Include activities that show any interesting skills mastered and the ability to persevere with a task. In addition, activities that illustrate leadership qualities, people skills, and community service can present your student as an asset to society and, if admitted, to their campus. Your three ring binder is a good place to keep award and activity memorabilia to jog your memory when college application time comes.

2. *any outside documentation of course work taken outside your home.* If your student has taken any advanced placement tests, CLEP exams, courses from a correspondence school, or early college credits, include this documentation.

3. *course descriptions.* Course descriptions are sometimes requested as back-up documentation to a home school transcript. If you have used the contract format suggested in this book, this will not be a heart stopping experience.

4. *book lists.* Hopefully, this information also will be stored away in your three ring binder.

5. *portfolios.* A portfolio is the three ring binder you were encouraged to keep, only in miniature. Pick out samples of your student's finest written work, most significant awards, and pictures of his most impressive projects. Keep the portfolio short and sweet — and impressive. Check the home school section on the College Board Web site for their portfolio recommendations.

   Portfolios are sometimes encouraged as a replacement for a transcript. This may work fine with a small college that provides individual attention for each applicant. In a large school, handling thousands of applicants, it may be difficult to find someone who is not too busy to thoughtfully review your student's work. Use portfolios selectively.

This ends our discussion on mastering the many details involved in crediting, grading, and documenting a high school program. The next section, "Designing the Program," will discuss planning the four year course of study and suggest books and materials for implementing your program.

PART THREE

DESIGNING THE PROGRAM

PLANNING A PERSONALIZED COURSE OF STUDY

Now you and your teen are ready to plan his high school course of study. The rest of this book is a listing of possible courses, with book suggestions, for the high school years. Reading through this section will help you start making decisions on what courses your teen should take. Decisions should be made with the *High School Course and Credit Suggestions* (page 26) in mind.

Two forms will help you with your decision making. The *Four Year Study Plan* form will help you put on paper what courses need to be taken and which year will work best to take each one. When it is completed you will have a map directing you through all four years of high school.

After the four year plan has been decided, use the *One Year Study Plan* form to list one year's courses with their book or material requirements. It will essentially be a shopping list for the upcoming year. In addition, it can serve as an informal record of courses and book selections.

Included on the next two pages are examples of a completed *Four Year Study Plan* and *One Year Study Plan*. With a total of 29 credits, the sample *Four Year Study Plan* appears very ambitious. However, our student is receiving six of these credits for four years of private piano and daily Bible courses, activities which occur after school hours for many students.

Remember, these plans are for example purposes only. Your course and material selections will be individualized to meet the academic needs and career direction of your student, college requirements, and the home school requirements of your state. Blank copies of the *One Year Study Plan* and the *Four Year Study Plan* are in Appendix B. They may be reproduced.

Note: Consider obtaining an academic planning guide from your local high school. It can be helpful to see what they recommend for a four year high school plan because their recommendations will be in compliance with your state's requirements. It is also interesting to see the diversity in course offerings.

FOUR YEAR STUDY PLAN FOR <u>Amy Jones</u>

9th grade courses	Credit	10th grade courses	Credit
English I	1.00	English II	1.00
Algebra I	1.00	Geometry	1.00
World Geography	1.00	American History	1.00
Physical Science	1.00	Biology	1.00
Word Processing	1.00	Latin II	1.00
Latin I	1.00	Private Piano	1.00
Private Piano	1.00	Church History	0.50
Bible Survey	0.50	Home Economics	1.00
P.E. — aerobics tape	0.50	P.E. — walking program	0.50
		P.E. — tennis lessons	0.50
Total	**8.00**	**Total**	**8.50**

11th grade courses	Credit	12th grade courses	Credit
English III	1.00	English 1301 & 1302 (college dual credit)	1.00
Creative Writing	0.50	Consumer Math	1.00
Algebra II	1.00	Government	0.50
World History	1.00	Economics	0.50
Latin III	1.00	Geology	0.50
Private Piano	1.00	Astronomy	0.50
Speech	0.50	Private Piano	1.00
Bible Doctrines	0.50	Worldview Studies	0.50
		Health	0.50
Total	**6.50**	**Total**	**6.00**

Total Credits by Subject Area			
Bible	2.00	Computers	1.00
English	4.50	Foreign Language	3.00
Math	4.00	Fine Arts	4.50
Science	3.00	Health and P.E.	2.00
Social Studies	4.00	Misc. Electives	1.00

Four Year Total 29.00

Use *Course and Credit Suggestions* on page 26 to fill out a four year plan.

ONE YEAR STUDY PLAN

Name: __Amy Jones_____ Grade: _9th_ Year: _Ninth_

Course Title	TEXTS OR MATERIALS
English I:	
Grammar	*Jensen's Grammar 1-3*
Mechanics	*Jensen's Punctuation*
Composition	*Format Writing* — paragraph styles & 5 paragraph essays
Vocabulary	*Wordly Wise 3000 # 6*
Literature	*The Hobbit* with Progeny Press guide
Literature	*The Yearling* with Progeny Press guide
Algebra I	*Algebra I* — Saxon
World Geography	Make geography notebook:
	Map Outlines of the World — for map outlines
	Comprehensive World Reference Guide — for reports
	Internet — for country reports
	The Continents — puzzles
Physical Science	School of Tomorrow paces with videos
Word Processing	project course, use resources at home
Latin I	*The Latin Road to English Grammar*
Piano	no new book
Bible Survey	read through the Bible
Physical Education	aerobics tape

Notes:

COURSE INFORMATION

The following information is included with each title:

Course:	This is a descriptive title, not necessarily a title for recording on the transcript. See the box on page 78 for more information.
Grade(s):	recommended grade levels
Prerequisite:	what course (or courses) must be completed before beginning this course (eg. Algebra 1 must precede Algebra 2)
Textbook/living book:	suggested textbook(s) or living books — sometimes there will be several
Author and/or publisher:	the author and/or publisher of the recommended book
Teacher helps:	what support materials (teacher's manual, tests, worksheets, etc.) are available to help teach the course
Description:	a general description of the course or book

Courses are arranged by subject area with a rough progression from easiest to most difficult. Because every home school will make different choices as to the requirements of a course, an exact level of difficulty cannot be determined.

Remedial course suggestions are listed first. These courses represent skills that should have been mastered before high school. Until they are mastered it is difficult to proceed efficiently with high school level work.

When appropriate to the subject matter, independent reading courses appear next. Depending on the reading selections chosen, courses of this nature can be easy or rigorously college preparatory.

Courses of average and advanced difficulty come next. Often the same basic books will be recommended for both. Adding supplementary activity books or additional reading can raise the difficulty level of a course significantly, making it rigorously college preparatory.

Remember to match the difficulty of a course to the needs of the student. Courses of average difficulty would be appropriate for the student who is not college bound or the college bound student outside the area he will be emphasizing in college. An example would be the liberal arts student who struggles in math. A sequence of math courses that prepares him for college algebra will probably be all that is required. Calculus studies in high school will most likely not be necessary. An advanced level course would be best for the student capable of rigorous study in all areas or who is planning to major in this area in college.

Finally, the last course suggestions to be listed are miscellaneous elective choices.

Remember, there is nothing inspired about the course listing that follows. Many core course suggestions are based on personal or customer observations of different textbooks and their level of difficulty. Independent reading courses often use favorite living books worthy of a teen's time. Other elective courses may be based on skills that are important for everyone to master. As you browse through the course ideas, you will hopefully be motivated to create your own courses using favorite study-worthy books.

It is not my intention to give you thorough descriptions of all the different materials available. Rather, I will point to a few tried and true, readily available resources. For detailed descriptions of these and other products, see Cathy Duffy and Mary Pride's curriculum guides (see Appendix A). These excellent resources provide information about the many products available on the ever expanding home school market. Their in-depth reviews should help you locate the most suitable materials for your student.

Please note that credit recommendations have not been made. Your requirements and design of any particular course will determine the number of credits to award.

How Should a Course Be Titled?

As you read this course listing you will probably come across courses with titles quite different from any you took in high school. These titles are descriptive, to help you see the direction of a course. They are not necessarily meant to be the course title on your teen's transcript.

When a college looks at your teen's transcript they want reassurance that your teen has been well-prepared for the academic rigors of college. Both grades and course titles should provide that reassurance. The titles on core courses, such as algebra I, geometry, algebra II, biology, chemistry, etc., should signify that the basics have been taught. Creative titles here may raise doubts as to the content of your course. In other areas more descriptive titles might be helpful. For example, titles such as grammar and composition, American literature, etc. may be helpful in defining the content of those nebulously titled English I through English IV courses.

Creative titles may be most helpful with elective courses. Here a creative title may indicate dedicated pursuits that go well beyond the normal high school course of study. For example, a course titled constitutional law, *in addition* to the required government credit indicates that your teen is a serious political science student. As a general rule, use course titles to reassure admissions counselors that basic course work has been successfully completed and that noteworthy elective credit was also earned.

Perhaps creativity is used to its best purpose in your curriculum selection. An English course might include participation in a summer Shakespearean festival. An American history course might include a creative and enriching choice of living books and a visit to a historical reenactment. This top-quality creative course can be hidden under the mundane title "American history" if this would best convince an office of admissions that the basics were covered. As stated before, always use your freedom to your student's advantage.

In our course listing please note that independent reading courses are not necessarily complete courses. For example, the study of God course and the studies in theology may together represent ½ credit, based on time spent and books read. These two courses could be combined and recorded on the transcript as Bible doctrines.

How Can a Home School Parent Help the Struggling Student?

An increasing number of parents are home schooling students that were placed in public school classrooms where the instruction or grading was modified. Often the struggle has been poor reading skills. Sometimes additional one-on-one instruction in phonics will result in reading improvement. This book's section on English courses will give some possible materials for strengthening a student's reading, spelling, or grammar. In addition to English suggestions, the course listing also contains ideas for remedial materials in most core subjects. These materials are written on an easier reading level. Use these materials *while you work on remediating reading and other areas of difficulty.*

Although learning problems need to be remediated before a student can move ahead, bear in mind that a high school program based on remedial classes will most likely *not* prepare a teen for the GED or college entrance. Whenever possible a teen should be moved into standard classes as soon as he can academically handle it. The decision to home school means you are taking on the responsibility for the education (or lack of education) your struggling teen receives. With three of my own children having various levels of hearing impairment, I know the extra stresses these situations put on home schooling. I will offer some practical but heartfelt advice:

Pray for your teen. Ask for God's wisdom in finding the best ways to love your teen and help him reach his fullest potential. Pray for endurance for the task.

Educate yourself. Read books, talk to other parents, and consider joining NATHHAN, an organization for parents home schooling children with special needs. Seek counsel and sympathetic fellowship.

Consider seeking help from home school friendly professionals. Your local or state home school support groups may know of such professionals in your area. They can evaluate your student and educate you on how best to help him. Bear in mind that being parent, teacher, and therapist (with all the instruction and correction that comes with each role) can strain the relationship between parent and child. Hiring a tutor or therapist to do some of the remediation allows you to focus on being positive and supportive, while they do at least some of the correcting.

Be patient. Welcome every success, even if it comes at a slower pace than you desire. Press toward long term goals of successful adulthood and don't agonize when short term goals are not speedily achieved. Be an encouragement. He needs to know someone is on his side!

Finally, don't doubt yourself. No one loves your teen as much or is as anxious for his success as you. God in His wisdom has placed this child in your care. Remember that He has called you to the task and will not fail to equip you for it.

How Do We Keep Our Course of Study Realistic?

Many wonderful home school books and materials exist that seem to beg us to use them. Add to that the many things we feel our teen must know to be prepared for the future. Before long we have set goals so unrealistic that our school year cannot possibly succeed. How do we plan realistically?

First of all, setting criteria before the course begins can help you keep your goals realistic. The input of a seasoned home schooler who has already walked the high school path can be valuable. In addition, our spouses (who know us so well) can often discern when idealism out of control has created an impossible pile of challenging requirements! Our feet must be firmly planted in reality if we are going to plan a course that is neither too easy nor too challenging. While planning, we must remind ourselves of a few important facts.

Remind yourself that you do not have the expertise to do all subjects equally well. Know your weak areas and be especially careful when choosing materials for your teen in these subjects. Look for books or programs that require less parental involvement. In our home school, I have chosen to use science videos on the high school level. They may not be the most rigorous academically, but my teens definitely learn more from them than they would from me. We have also used our local junior college for advanced math courses.

In addition, remind yourself that you also have limited time. This is especially true if you have more than one student. You cannot be equally involved in every subject studied. Some courses will need to be done with a great deal of independence by your teen while others will require more of your attention. Vary your curriculum choices so that all do not require an intense time commitment from you.

It is always nice when the areas you study closely together are subjects both you and your teen love. Those experiences create special moments that make home schoolers positively glow. Unfortunately, it doesn't always work that way. It is not unusual for both you and your teen to dislike or struggle with the same subject. Often you must be involved closely or it will not get done. Choose the least painful material for both of you, hire a tutor, or join a home school co-op class. God will reward your faithfulness.

Finally, high school is a wonderful time for extensive reading. The key is a careful selection of reading material. Know which books should be discussed to fully benefit from them and which do not require your close interaction. Vary your selections with this in mind. I have heard it quoted that the best way to prepare for successful college studies is to read widely and read well. That is a goal easily met through home schooling.

What Makes a Course of Study Christian?

How do we make our studies Christian? God's Word admonishes us in I Corinthian 10:31, "Therefore, whether you eat or drink, or whatever you do, do all to the glory of God." This verse provides a good basis for answering that question.

Christian education does not require using textbooks that put a Bible verse on the bottom of each page. It does not require using examples from the Bible to teach sentence diagramming or math concepts. Using these resources is certainly fine, *unless* they become your definition of Christian education. True Christian education nurtures a godly condition of the heart.

We are to live our lives with a constant awareness that "we are not our own, that we have been bought with a price." A life lived with this awareness is lived to the glory of God. All of life has become sacred, and so has schooling.

Learning to read becomes sacred as it equips us to more clearly hear God speak to us through Scripture and prepares us to enjoy the beauty of God's gift of language. Science becomes sacred as we study the handiwork of the Creator. Learning multiplication tables becomes sacred when we realize they work in an orderly fashion because they reflect the character of our wise Creator God. Every school subject and all of life becomes a character curriculum when done faithfully and cheerfully unto the Lord. Each subject studied should progressively reveal God's power and control over His universe. With God's grace, this growing awareness will result in an obedient Christian walk.

In contrast, any subject can become an unholy offering to God. Even Bible reading when grumbled through dishonors God. Bible verses at the bottom of a textbook page cannot Christianize an education if the heart is rebellious or cold.

The Westminster Shorter Catechism's first question is, "What is the chief end of man?" The answer is, "Man's chief end is to glorify God and enjoy Him forever." Schooling pursued with this heart desire is Christian education and bears fruit for God's kingdom. May we as home schoolers display this holy purpose as we pursue excellence in all we do.

BIBLE AND CHARACTER DEVELOPMENT COURSES

Although biblical studies would most likely not be considered in a secular high school, for the Christian home schooler they should be foundational. The greatest contribution we can make towards our teen's future is a vibrant Christian faith. Nothing else is eternal.

Any biblical studies plan should contain systematic Bible reading. I strongly encourage you to implement a plan for reading through the Scriptures, hopefully more than once during the high school years. There are many plans for doing this. Some are just a schedule sheet where the daily reading is checked off when completed. Another possibility is the *One Year Bible* which divides the Bible into daily readings.

In addition to ongoing Bible reading I would recommend other areas of biblical studies. Church history teaches students that Christianity is much bigger than themselves, their parents, and the churches they attend. In both our American and home school individualism, we have too often neglected our connection to the corporate body of Christ, both in the world today and in previous centuries. Salvation is not just a private matter; it places each of us into a family which transcends time and place. Today we stand on the shoulders of God's faithful servants who have preceded us into eternity. Introduce your teen and yourself, perhaps for the first time, to these heroes. Church history suggestions can be found on pages 128-130.

Another important area is worldview studies. Worldview studies will help your teen understand both his Christian faith and the underlying premises of philosophies opposed to Christianity. Worldview courses are listed in the social studies course listing, but could be considered Bible, philosophy, or social studies electives.

Browse through the course suggestions and consider adding a few as electives to your teen's course of study. All books recommended for Bible or character development courses adhere to the basic tenets of the historic Christian faith.

BIBLE ELECTIVES

| *Course:* **Bible Reading** | *Grade:* **9-12** | *Prerequisite:* **none** |

Daily Bible reading plan or
The One Year Bible, Tyndale
The Victor Journey through the Bible, V. Gilbert Beers
▸ Teacher helps: independent reading course, no teacher helps needed
▸ Description: A systematic reading through the entire Bible. Arranged chronologically, *The Victor Journey through the Bible* includes interesting cultural information to enrich the study.

| *Course:* **Bible Study** (for the serious Bible student) | *Grade:* **9-12** | *Prerequisite:* **none** |

Knowing Scripture, R.C. Sproul
The Reformation Study Bible, Thomas Nelson Publishers
The Victor Journey through the Bible, V. Gilbert Beers
▸ Teacher helps: independent reading course, no teacher helps needed
▸ Description: R.C. Sproul's book gives a good overview on how to study the Bible effectively. The notes in *The Reformation Study Bible* (New King Jame version) are written by dependable Bible scholars; R.C. Sproul was the general editor. Arranged chronologically, *The Victor Journey through the Bible* includes interesting cultural information to enrich the study.

| *Course:* **Study of God** | *Grade:* **9-12** | *Prerequisite:* **none** |

Knowing God, J.I. Packer
A Heart for God, Sinclair Ferguson
The Attributes of God, A.W. Pink
The Holiness of God, R.C. Sproul
▸ Teacher helps: independent reading course, no teacher helps needed
▸ Description: A Biblical study on the character of God. Understanding His character is foundational to every Christian's faith. All of these books would make excellent choices.

| *Course:* **Christian Apologetics** | *Grade:* **11-12** | *Prerequisite:* **none** |

Can Man Live without God, Ravi Zacharias
Jesus among Other Gods, Ravi Zacharias
Deliver Us from Evil, Ravi Zacharias
▸ Teacher helps: independent reading course, no teacher helps needed
▸ Description: Ravi Zacharias is an articulate, thought-provoking defender of the Christian faith. Many of his messages and seminars can be purchased in video or audio formats.

| *Course:* **God's Sovereignty in Suffering** | *Grade:* **9-12** | *Prerequisite:* **none** |

When God Weeps, Joni Erickson Tada/Steven Estes
▸ Teacher helps: independent reading course, no teacher helps needed
▸ Description: It is difficult to see God's children suffer. It is especially difficult when it is a family member, a close friend, or ourselves. This well-written, deeply meaningful book explains God's purposes in man's suffering. Joni Erickson Tada and Steven Estes are well-qualified to speak on the subject.

Course: **Studies in Theology**   *Grade:* **9-12**   *Prerequisite:* **none**

Choose one:

Essential Truths of the Christian Faith, R.C. Sproul

Concise Theology: A Guide to Historic Christian Beliefs, J.I. Packer

▶ Teacher helps: independent reading course, no teacher helps needed

▶ Description: Both of these readable books will provide the student with a strong foundation in the major tenets of the Christian faith.

Course: **Christian Growth**   *Grade:* **9-12**   *Prerequisite:* **none**

Basic Christianity, John R. Stott

Profiting from the Word, A.W. Pink

The Cost of Discipleship, Dietrich Bonhoeffer

▶ Teacher helps: independent reading course, no teacher helps needed

▶ Description: A study designed to aid in personal growth through an understanding of the work of Christ, the value of the Word of God, and discipleship.

Course: **The History of Christianity**   *Grade:* **9-12**   *Prerequisite:* **none**

Sketches from Church History, S.M. Houghton, Banner of Truth, publishers

▶ Teacher helps: independent reading course, no teacher helps needed

▶ Description: An excellent study of the Christian Church through the ages providing the student information on the richness of his spiritual heritage.

Course: **Classic Christian Reading**   *Grade:* **9-12**   *Prerequisite:* **none**

The City of God or *Confessions of St. Augustine*, Augustine

Imitation of Christ, Thomas a' Kempis

Bondage of the Will, Martin Luther

Institutes of the Christian Religion, John Calvin, (in one volume, Tony Lane editor)

Pilgrim's Progress, John Bunyan

▶ Teacher helps: independent reading course, no teacher helps needed

▶ Description: This is a challenging independent study for the serious Bible and church history student. All of the selections represent books that have had a far-reaching effect on the history of the Christian Church. *The City of God* profoundly affected the reformers hundreds of years after its publication. *Confessions* is the testimony of Augustine's conversion. *The Imitation of Christ*, perhaps the most widely read Christian devotional book in the world for the past 500 years, is both simple and moving. Luther's *The Bondage of the Will* and Calvin's *Institutes* were the great reformers' most influential works. *Pilgrim's Progress* remains a widely read Christian classic.

Course: **Readings in C. S. Lewis (or . . .)**   *Grade:* **9-12**   *Prerequisite:* **none**

▶ Teacher helps: independent reading course, no teacher helps needed

▶ Description: An independent study concentrating on an individual author's work. Although I highly recommend C. S. Lewis, you may want to consider G. K. Chesterton, Martyn Lloyd-Jones, A.W. Pink, Francis Schaeffer, Charles Spurgeon, and A.W. Tozier. In addition, there are many popular modern choices, such as: Charles Colson, Sinclair Ferguson, John MacArthur, J.I. Packer, John Piper, R.C. Sproul, Chuck Swindoll, and Ravi Zacharias.

CHARACTER DEVELOPMENT

Course: **Godly Character for Young Men**   *Grade:* **9-12**   *Prerequisite:* **none**

Thoughts for Young Men, J.C. Ryle
The Mark of a Man, Elisabeth Elliot
Passion and Purity, Elisabeth Elliot
choose a dating/courtship book (see Dating/Courtship below)
▸ Teacher helps: independent reading course, no teacher helps needed
▸ Description: A study designed to help young men develop character that is pleasing in the sight of God.

Course: **Godly Character for Young Women**   *Grade:* **9-12**   *Prerequisite:* **none**

Let Me Be a Woman, Elisabeth Elliot
Passion and Purity, Elisabeth Elliot
choose a dating/courtship book (see Dating/Courtship below)
▸ Teacher helps: independent reading course, no teacher helps needed
▸ Description: A study designed to help young women develop character that is pleasing in the sight of God.

Course: **Dating/Courtship**   *Grade:* **9-12**   *Prerequisite:* **none**

Dating with Integrity, John Holzmann
I Kissed Dating Good-bye, Josh Harris
Boy Meets Girl, Josh Harris
Passion and Purity, Elisabeth Elliot
When Dreams Come True, Eric Ludy
When God Writes Your Love Story, Eric Ludy
▸ Teacher helps: independent reading course, no teacher helps needed
▸ Description: Some excellent books are available on this topic now. Different views of dating and courtship are shared, but all have the common goal of promoting purity before marriage. You may want to pre-read these titles. The stories aren't only about remaining pure before marriage; sometimes they are also about God's reclamation after a fall into sin.

ENGLISH COURSES

God holds language in high esteem. With the entire universe at His disposal, He chose the printed word as a primary means of communicating His loving plan of redemption to man. As His image bearers (marred though the image is) we should follow God's example. A thoughtful and careful honing of communication skills shows that we also hold language in an elevated position. Let's examine these skills one by one.

Grammar is the study of word usage. Our earliest grammar study begins as infants and toddlers learning to speak. Parents who model correct speech in their everyday conversation have given their children a decided advantage in learning grammar skills. It is always easier to learn something correctly from the beginning than to try to correct wrong usage once it's imbedded in the memory. During elementary school, students begin learning the different parts of speech: nouns, pronouns, verbs, adjectives, adverbs, prepositions, conjunctions, and interjections. As the student progresses through his school years, he will learn increasingly complex rules that govern the proper use of each part of speech.

Mechanics includes the study of other details necessary for successful writing, primarily capitalization and punctuation. Most grammar books also cover mechanics. Like grammar, this study begins in the elementary grades and continues until mastered.

Some home schoolers finish formal grammar and mechanics studies in the ninth grade. A writing handbook would then become a constant reference when grammatical or mechanical problems arise. However, if desired, it is also possible to use grammar workbooks, such as those from A Beka or Bob Jones University Press, through all four high school grades.

The end result of all this study is (hopefully!) students that can use language with great skill both in speaking and writing. This is best achieved by practically applying these skills to the regular writing of compositions along with some opportunity for public speaking.

Composition is the art of expressing oneself in writing. It includes learning the various standard formats for constructing sentences, paragraphs, and larger works. It also involves developing a personal style of writing. High school level composition will show the most progress if grammatical and mechanical skills are already well-developed.

While overlap exists, there are two basic directions within the study of composition: creative and informational writing. At their best, both types of writing bring glory to God. We will look briefly at each.

Creative writing offers the greatest freedom for personal expression through the writing of poetry, short stories, novels, plays, etc. At its best it makes us laugh, cry, or wonder at its beauty. Creative writing is not only creative expression. It also includes learning effective formats for each of the different writing genres.

Informational or expository writing organizes ideas, information, or processes. This promotion of order helps daily life flow more smoothly. It includes countless day to day writing tasks. In the home it means writing grocery lists, recipes, letters to friends, and a letter to the editor. In the business world it includes writing business letters, resumes, e-mail correspondence, employee directives, and speeches. In school it includes learning the formats for proper paragraphing (vital for essay questions on tests), research papers, book reports, and speech writing.

Not all students will choose to write creatively. However, everyone is required in life to write informationally. How do these thoughts direct us in making academic choices for our students? Consider putting the greatest composition efforts into learning the writing formats necessary for success in the academic and business world. For those students more creatively gifted, an elective course in creative writing could be offered. Check the course listing for some excellent resources.

Dictionary and research skills include learning the proper use of the tools needed for study. These tools would include the dictionary, encyclopedia, the library classification systems (Dewey Decimal and Library of Congress), and various common reference works found in libraries. Using these library tools, the student should learn how to search for appropriate books and magazines on the topic he is pursuing. It is also necessary to know how to navigate the Internet and its vast resources with ease. Dictionary and research skills are not always a separate area of study. The completion of several research projects can often teach these skills adequately.

Vocabulary is the study of word meanings. This study is preceded by a focus on spelling during the elementary grades. After the sixth grade it is not unusual for the emphasis to switch to vocabulary development. Some students are not ready for this switch. If your older student has not mastered spelling it is important to revisit this skill while continuing ahead with vocabulary. Keep the future in mind. In the work force poor spelling can make someone appear illiterate, regardless of how well they read and how hard they work. Although spell checks are great, they will not be available for every writing situation on the job. And they are not always accurate!

There are different ways to approach the study of vocabulary. Vocabulary words can be drawn from the literature, history, and science being studied. They can also be studied through separate vocabulary workbooks. A very thorough program may include both. For the college bound student, a study of Latin or Greek roots is an appropriate addition to vocabulary studies. Studying roots, or the foreign language itself, can greatly enhance scores on college entrance exams.

Literature involves reading and analyzing written works that have shown themselves of lasting value through the test of time. It will include studying the elements contained in the different literary genres. For example, studying short stories or novels will include an examination of setting, characterizations, types of conflict, etc. Essays might be examined for persuasive devices used and the possible presence of propaganda techniques.

With so much available to read, how do you choose where to concentrate your efforts? Actually, it is amazing how much agreement there is on what literature is truly great. There are many lists and reading plans available. This book includes lists of American, English, and world literature upon whose lasting value there is a consensus. There is, however, a limit to how many whole books can be read in four years. Should you prefer a wider exposure to more literary choices, A Beka and Bob Jones University Press publish high school literature books. These books concentrate on poems, short stories, and excerpts from longer works. An anthology of this nature is especially helpful in providing a historical overview of a literary time period.

A prerequisite to literature studies is well-developed reading skills. In fact, strong reading skills are necessary for success in every academic subject and almost any future career. If your student struggles in reading, I strongly encourage you to continue working on reading skills. The literature course listing includes some suggestions for remedial reading.

Putting the Puzzle Together

Now that we've looked at all the pieces of the English puzzle, let's look at different ways to put it together. This is where you and your student's personality, future goals, and your present situation must all be examined when making a decision. There are three basic approaches, all academically sound:

1. Use a worktext approach, such as Alpha Omega or School of Tomorrow, where all the skills are integrated into one set of worktexts. This is the easiest approach for the parent. No juggling required!

2. Choose materials from one publisher such as Bob Jones University Press or A Beka Books. They may have separate grammar, literature, and vocabulary books to juggle, but the different components of their program will share the same educational philosophy and work well with each other.

3. Choose different materials to teach each skill separately. This is undoubtedly the most difficult way to proceed, but also the most flexible. Possible reasons for integrating your English program yourself include the desire:

♦ to use a favorite program that only covers one particular skill.
♦ to work at different levels in different skills.
♦ to choose composition topics that integrate with other subjects.
♦ to teach dictionary and research skills through practical use.
♦ to study Latin as a foreign language rather than using a vocabulary text.
♦ to choose literature that integrates with your history studies.
♦ to study literature through the use of whole books instead of excerpts.

Elements of an English Program

If you choose to integrate your English program yourself, you will need to decide how to order the teaching of skills. Following is a possible timetable for teaching the various English skills.

9th grade	emphasize grammar, mechanics, include short compositions, some vocabulary, read a few novels, begin studying the elements of literature
10th grade	use an English handbook when grammar or mechanical problems arise, increase length and variety of compositions, for the college bound study Greek and Latin roots for vocabulary, increase the amount of literature studied, continue studying the elements of literature
11th grade	continue to refer to English handbook as needed, increase length and variety of compositions, for the college bound continue with vocabulary work perhaps using an SAT or ACT preparation guide in addition to studying Greek and Latin roots, include a historical anthology of literature (American?) and study several novels
12th grade	continue to refer to English handbook as needed, increase length and variety of compositions, continue vocabulary work (can use words in literature), include a historical anthology of literature (British or world?) and study several novels

If including all these elements in your English program is overwhelming, don't panic. Instead, make some adaptations. Consider the following ideas:

1. Divide your areas of English study into semesters. Example: first semester study grammar, mechanics, and composition. Second semester study vocabulary, literature, and write book reports. This timetable could be further divided into quarters, emphasizing different skills at different times.

2. Study different skills on different days of the week.

3. If your teen has already mastered an area (like grammar or mechanics), don't restudy. Instead use an English handbook as a reference when problems arise.

4. Carry some work into the next school year if necessary.

5. Adapt the amount of work required according to the abilities and future ambitions of each student.

Communication skills are important in most career fields. Therefore, the mastery of English should be emphasized for all students. For that reason you may want to keep your English courses fairly ambitious.

A listing of possible resources for some of the English skills we have discussed begins on page 92 (no separate dictionary and research suggestions are offered). Remedial suggestions are included under the appropriate headings (examples: spelling with vocabulary, reading with literature). A book report form, a list of self-editing questions, and a checklist for a research paper are included after the composition resources. American, British, and world literature book choices follow the literature section. When Christian study guides are available, that is also noted.

The final entry under English contains sample standard and advanced English classes for all four years. Please do not burden yourself by trying to follow these suggestions exactly. Instead, interact with them as you set your own expectations. I have not included sample remedial classes. The format of remedial courses should be based on the immediate needs of each individual student. Remember that remedial materials are generally not considered high school level; use your own discretion how to best incorporate them into your program.

In literature you will find recommendations for the number of books to read. Consider these minimal numbers. The more your teen reads, the greater will be his academic success. Both reading and writing skills improve with exposure to good literature. If you would like additional reading suggestions, two books worth consulting are Terry Glaspey's *Great Books of the Christian Tradition* or *Invitation to the Classics* by Louise Cowan and Os Guinness.

What English Reference Books Are Most Helpful?

First of all, every student needs a good dictionary. Both the *Merriam Webster Collegiate Dictionary* and the *Webster's Third Edition New International Dictionary* are considered authoritative by the *Chicago Manual of Style*. In addition, many home schoolers appreciate the *Webster's 1828 Dictionary*. Its use can be an interesting lesson in the fluidity (not always for the better) of the English language, but it will not be very helpful with modern English standards. In fact, English can change so rapidly that the dictionary you used as a child may not give accurate help.

A thesaurus is another valuable tool for any writer. A thesaurus provides synonym and antonym help. For students it is a helpful means of increasing their vocabulary and improving the variety of word choice in their writing. (People over forty find it helpful when the right word can't quite escape their brain!) If you don't have a thesaurus, both *Roget's International Thesaurus* and *Rodale's Synonym Finder* are good choices.

An English handbook is the next important item. The answers to questions concerning grammar, punctuation, capitalization, and other language mechanics can be found quickly. A Beka Books, Bob Jones University Press, and Rod and Staff Publishers all have handbooks that are widely used by home schoolers.

Finally, no writer's bag of tricks would be complete without Strunk and White's *The Elements of Style*. This small book contains succinct help for improving writing.

GRAMMAR AND MECHANICS

English Skill: Remedial Grammar   Grade: **9-12***   Prerequisite: **none**

*The earlier remediation begins, the better.

Winston Grammar, Precious Memories

▸ Teacher helps: everything needed is in the kit

▸ Description: In *Winston Grammar* cue cards use picture clues and short phrases to describe parts of speech and noun functions. Each lesson begins with the teacher writing out sample sentences which the student analyzes using the cue cards learned thus far. A student workbook follows up the lesson with sentences which the student marks using a simple system as an alternative to diagramming. If this approach works well for you *Advanced Winston Grammar* is also available.

English Skill: Remedial Grammar   Grade: **9-12***   Prerequisite: **none**

*The earlier remediation begins, the better.

Rules of the Game, EPS

▸ Teacher helps: three answer keys

▸ Description: A set of three workbooks that help students discover the grammar rules through a series of questions and examples. Written for junior high, it might be appropriate for the remedial high school student.

English Skill: Remedial Grammar & Mechanics   Grade: **9-12***   Prerequisite: **none**

*The earlier remediation begins, the better.

Easy Grammar Level I or
Easy Grammar Plus, Isha

▸ Teacher helps: teacher's manual

▸ Description: *Easy Grammar* is a large fill-in-the-blank workbook teaching parts of speech, punctuation, and capitalization. Prepositions are taught first. The student memorizes them so he can successfully eliminate prepositional phrases from sentences, making it easier to find the simple sentence and its parts. *Easy Grammar's* various books begin with *Easy Grammar 3 & 4* (third and fourth grade) and progress to *Easy Grammar Plus* for high school. All build on each other. *Easy Grammar Level I* is a junior high book, making it appropriate for remedial work, although *Easy Grammar Plus* used at a slower pace may also work fine since it is easier than many grammars. The teacher's manual contains the answers and blank student pages which may be photocopied, although purchasing the separate student workbook is usually more cost effective than photocopying. I hope someday they will put out a teacher's manual with only answers — it would be more cost effective for the home schooler.

English Skill: Remedial Grammar & Mechanics   Grade: **9-12***   Prerequisite: **none**

*The earlier remediation begins, the better.

English Worksheets, Rod and Staff

▸ Teacher helps: teacher's edition

▸ Description: This is a series of three workbooks covering parts of speech, the sentence, and punctuation and capitalization. They are inexpensive and uncomplicated.

English Skill: Grammar and Mechanics   Grade: **9-12**   Prerequisite: **none**

Editor in Chief C1, C2, EPS

▸ Teacher helps: student workbook, answers in back

▸ Description: *Editor in Chief* teaches the student to sharpen his editing skills by finding the errors contained in the reading selection for each lesson. (If working below high school level, books A1, A2, or B1, B2 could be used.)

English Skill: **Grammar and Mechanics**	*Grade:* **9-12**	*Prerequisite:* **none**

Easy Grammar Plus, Isha

▶ Teacher helps: teacher's manual

▶ Description: *Easy Grammar* is a large fill-in-the-blank workbook teaching parts of speech, punctuation, and capitalization. Prepositions are taught first. The student memorizes them so he can successfully eliminate prepositional phrases from sentences, making it easier to find the simple sentence and its parts. The teacher's manual contains the answers and blank student pages which may be photocopied, although purchasing the separate student workbook is usually more cost effective than photocopying. I hope someday they will put out a teacher's manual with only answers — it would be more cost effective for the home schooler.

English Skill: **Grammar and Mechanics**	*Grade:* **9-12**	*Prerequisite:* **none**

Jensen's Grammar, Volumes 1-3; Jensen's Punctuation, Wordsmith

▶ Teacher helps: student workbooks, key in back

▶ Description: *Jensen's Grammar* is a thorough one year program that should effectively polish off your high school grammar program. *Jensen's Punctuation* (a newly combined edition of *Major Punctuation* and *General Punctuation*) is also thorough in its coverage of punctuation. There is plenty of opportunity for practice in these consumable workbooks.

English Skill: **Grammar and Mechanics**	*Grade:* **9-12**	*Prerequisite:* **none**

Writing and Grammar, Bob Jones University Press

▶ Teacher helps: two-part teacher's manual

▶ Description: Grades 7-9 have been recently revised. Contents include grammar, library and study skills, and instruction and assignments for honing writing skills. "Part One" of the teacher's guide contains teaching and scheduling helps and workbook answers. "Part Two" contains reproducible worksheets and helps for objectively grading compositions. Grades 10-12, still in first edition at the time I am writing this, has everything contained in one teacher's guide.

COMPOSITION

English Skill: **Composition**	*Grade:* **7-12**	*Prerequisite:* **none**

Composition Lifepac Select, Alpha Omega

▶ Teacher helps: teacher's guide

▶ Description: Alpha Omega *Select* electives are lifepacs topically chosen to create a one semester course. Since the course includes both junior high and high school level lifepacs, it will be less challenging than some other choices.

English Skill: **Composition**	*Grade:* **all grades**	*Prerequisite:* **none**

Teaching Writing: Structure and Style, The Institute for Excellence in Writing

▶ Teacher helps: videos, syllabus, no student workbook

▶ Description: Andrew Pudewa has a unique methodology for teaching both creative and expository writing to all age levels. The videos let you sit in on class as he teaches adults how to use his methods. Additional videos show him working with children in various age groups. His note-taking techniques are valuable for learning summarization skills, organizing writing, and avoiding plagiarism. They can be used for both oral or written presentations. His stylistic techniques teach objective methods for improving the creativity of sentence structure. The information presented in the videos is also in the accompanying syllabus. Although pricey, this program sets a great foundation for any type of writing.

Composition (cont'd)

English Skill: **Composition**   *Grade:* **10-12**   *Prerequisite:* **none**

Wordsmith Craftsman, Janie Cheaney, Common Sense Press
▸ Teacher helps: none needed
▸ Description: *Wordsmith Craftsman* polishes practical writing skills. These skills include taking notes, outlining, letters, summaries, reports, paragraphing, writing techniques, and various forms of essays. Janie Cheaney directly addresses the student using her delightful writing style.

English Skill: **Composition**   *Grade:* **9-12**   *Prerequisite:* **none**

Format Writing, Frode Jensen, Wordsmith
▸ Teacher helps: none needed
▸ Description: *Format Writing* can be successfully used through all four years of high school composition. Formats taught include types of paragraphing, five paragraph papers, pre'cis (summarizations), and research papers.

English Skill: **Composition**   *Grade:* **9-12**   *Prerequisite:* **none**

Writing Strands, David Marks, National Writing Institute
▸ Teacher helps: none needed, student-directed
▸ Description: *Writing Strands* is a series of thin, spiral-bound books, which gradually move the student through all the necessary writing skills. High schoolers will begin anywhere from "Level Four" on up, depending on their previous composition experience. Both creative and expository writing are taught. The books directly address the student. Teacher involvement will be correcting and discussing compositions.

English Skill: **Research Paper Writing**   *Grade:* **9-12**   *Prerequisite:* **none**

Writing a Research Paper, Edward J. Shewan, Christian Liberty Press
▸ Teacher helps: none needed, student-directed
▸ Description: This little inexpensive booklet provides an excellent nutshell presentation of writing a research paper.

English Skill: **Creative Writing**   *Grade:* **7-12**   *Prerequisite:* **none**

Wordsmith, Janie Cheaney, *Common Sense Press*
▸ Teacher helps: teacher's guide
▸ Description: Another excellent guide for creative writing, geared to students junior high and up. Written directly to the student, the writing is both concise and entertaining. It would make an excellent elective course. The teacher's guide includes teaching and scheduling helps.

English Skill: **Short Story Writing**   *Grade:* **10-12**   *Prerequisite:* **none**

The Exciting World of Creative Writing, Ruth McDaniels, Christian Liberty Press
▸ Teacher helps: none required
▸ Description: An excellent guide which carefully walks the student through the process of writing a short story. This friendly and encouraging book contains a wealth of information for the budding writer. Consider using it for an elective course in creative writing.

BOOK REPORT FORMAT

NAME _____   DATE_____

TITLE: (underlined or in italics)

AUTHOR:

PUBLISHER:

COPYRIGHT YEAR:

BOOK TYPE: (biography, fiction, historical fiction, short story, nonfiction, Christian fiction, etc.)

SETTING: Tell where and when the story takes place.

SUMMARY: Write at least one paragraph of five or six sentences summarizing the plot.

CHARACTER SKETCH: Choose one character to describe. Look for both positive and negative characteristics. How did these characteristics affect the action of the book?

THEME: What do you believe is the overall theme or moral of this book? What do you think the author was trying to say or teach?

RECOMMENDATION: Would you recommend this book? Tell why or why not.

General Editing Questions

YES	NO	
		Did I write with my reader in mind?
		Did I follow my outline or organizational plan?
		Can the reader follow my thought progression easily?
		Have I used strong nouns and verbs?
		Have I used adjectives and adverbs lightly?
		Have I selected the best words for my purposes rather than the most impressive?
		Are there any unnecessary words I can leave out? Check sentence by sentence.
		Did I show not tell? (Ex: "Her lip quivered," *not* "she began to cry.")
		Have I varied my sentence lengths?
		Is the writing style I'm using natural for me?
		Is my final draft free of spelling, punctuation, and grammar mistakes?
		Self-editing has its limitations. Am I brave enough to give my paper to someone else to critique?
		Does my final polished copy glorify God both in content and presentation?
Additional editing hints for an excellent paper. Have you:		
		Read it very slowly out loud, word by word? You'll catch more errors.
		Used a different color ink to mark the errors you find? Red shows best.
		Read it through different times looking for different problems? Ex. Read it once for spelling, once for punctuation, once for word clarity, etc.)
		Learned how to use a word processing program on your computer? It makes editing much easier.
		Started fresh with a clean copy after making your initial corrections in order to catch more mistakes? If the paper gets too messy with corrections, you can no longer see additional errors. On a clean copy errors you missed may jump out at you!
		Be on the look out for repetitive errors.

Phil. 4:8: Whatever things are true, whatever things are noble, whatever things are just, whatever things are pure, whatever things are lovely, whatever things are of good report, if there is any virtue and if there is anything praiseworthy meditate (editor's note: and write!) on these things.

Research Paper Checklist

Check off and date when each assignment is completed.   Paper due on:

✓	Date	Assignment
		Week One
		I. Preliminary reading on research papers. (Consider *Format Writing,* the section on major papers or *Writing a Research Paper* by CLP.)
		II. Gather information. Use guidelines in above publications for cards.
		A. Keep a bibliography card for each source.
		B. Read and collect information on note cards about your topic.
		C. Turn in for evaluation.
		III. Organize information.
		A. Separate note cards into topical piles.
		B. Write your outline using your note card piles as your guide.
		C. Turn in for evaluation.
		Week Two
		IV. Write your rough draft. Follow your outline, refer to note cards, and be sure to include in-text citations as you go.) Include:
		A. An introductory paragraph with a thesis sentence.
		B. Body paragraphs.
		C. A conclusion paragraph which directs the reader back to the thesis sentence or recaps main points.
		D. Organize "Works Cited" page.
		E. Use a "Bibliography" page for additional reading not cited in the paper.
		V. Put the paper up for several days and forget about it.
		Week Three
		VI. With a fresh mind polish your rough draft looking for the following errors:
		A. Errors in structure
		1. Not following your outline.
		2. Disorderly sequence of thoughts within a paragraph.

Research Paper Checklist (continued)

Check off and date when each assignment is completed.

✓	Date	Assignment
		B. Errors in style
		1. Wordiness — Ask yourself:
		a. *What sentences or phrases can I take out and not miss?*
		b. *What words are unnecessarily difficult when a simpler word will do?*
		2. Ambiguity — Ask yourself:
		a. *Is this the clearest way to say this?*
		b. *Will my audience understand this?*
		C. Errors in mechanics — Check for errors in:
		1. Spelling
		2. Punctuation
		3. Sentence fragments
		4. Run-on sentences
		5. Grammar
		D. Errors in form — Follow the format rules taught in your preliminary reading for the following items:
		1. Title page
		2. Body of paper
		a. double space
		b. include in-text citations
		3. Works cited page
		4. Bibliography page, if included
		VI. Complete second draft and turn in for evaluation.
		Week Four
		VII. Make corrections suggested and resubmit in final form for grading.

Additional Notes:

VOCABULARY

| *English Skill:* **Remedial Spelling** | *Grade:* **9-12*** | *Prerequisite:* **none** |

*The earlier remediation begins, the better.

Spelling Power, Castlemoyle Books
- ▶ Teacher helps: everything needed is in the teacher's book, student record books available.
- ▶ Description: *Spelling Power* begins with diagnostic tests that will help you place your student at the appropriate level in the spelling lists. The student contracts each week to use some of the many activities given for reinforcing the spelling words. A checksheet presents a systematic routine for studying the words based on visual memory — a skill often lacking in poor spellers.

| *English Skill:* **Vocabulary** | *Grade:* **6-9** | *Prerequisite:* **none** |

Vocabu-Lit, Perfection Learning Company
- ▶ Teacher helps: teacher's editions
- ▶ Description: *Vocabu-Lit* is a literature-based vocabulary series for grades 6-9. Excerpts from classic stories, novels, poems, essays, and speeches provide the words to study. In addition to the answers, teacher helps include a glossary, dictionary of vocabulary words, and a comprehensive word list. I hope in time this series extends through all four high school years.

| *English Skill:* **Vocabulary** | *Grade:* **7-12** | *Prerequisite:* **none** |

Vocabulary: Level A-F, Bob Jones University Press
- ▶ Teacher helps: teacher's edition
- ▶ Description: Areas studied over the course of the series include Latin and Greek prefixes and roots, words borrowed from other languages, using context to discover word meaning, proper word selection to enhance writing, and terminology pertinent to vocabulary studies. If you have not previously done vocabulary studies you may want to start with Level A to get the full benefit of this series.

| *English Skill:* **Vocabulary** | *Grade:* **9-12** | *Prerequisite:* **none** |

Wordly Wise 3000 #6-9, Educator's Publishing Service
- ▶ Teacher helps: answer key
- ▶ Description: *Wordly Wise* is a vocabulary series that has long been popular with home schoolers. *Wordly Wise 3000* contains the same helpful variety of activities as the original series with the added feature of using a short narrative to study the vocabulary words in context. Some words are included that frequently appear on SAT tests. An inexpensive answer key is also available.

| *English Skill:* **Vocabulary** | *Grade:* **7-11** | *Prerequisite:* **none** |

Vocabulary from Classical Roots, Educator's Publishing Service
- ▶ Teacher helps: answer key
- ▶ Description: Latin and Greek roots studied through a variety of exercises. Valuable for enriching vocabulary and for SAT preparation.

| *English Skill:* **Vocabulary** | *Grade:* **9-12** | *Prerequisite:* **none** |

Latin I and II, Greek I, Frode Jensen, Wordsmith
- ▶ Teacher helps: answers in back of book
- ▶ Description: Each challenging book in this series contains a master list of Latin or Greek prefixes, roots, and suffixes. Using this list, students dissect an English word into parts, searching for its meaning in the original language. They then apply this knowledge to choosing a current definition from the list provided. The approach is challenging, requiring careful thought and analysis. It should make excellent SAT/ACT preparation.

READING AND LITERATURE

| *English Skill:* **Remedial Reading** | *Grade:* **9-12*** | *Prerequisite:* **none** |

*The earlier remediation begins, the better.

Alpha Phonics, Samuel Blumenfeld, Paradigm Company

▶ Teacher helps: suggested lessons in back of book

▶ Description: Samuel Blumenfeld was an early activist in promoting a return to phonics. His *Alpha Phonics* provides a simple no-nonsense drill for practicing phonics skills. Teacher preparation is located in the back of the book and is simple and straightforward.

| *English Skill:* **Remedial Reading** | *Grade:* **9-12*** | *Prerequisite:* **none** |

*The earlier remediation begins, the better.

Phonics Tutor, software, reader, and workbook, 4:20 Communications

▶ Teacher helps: teacher's manual

▶ Description: *Phonics Tutor* is a computer program with a thorough and systematic presentation of phonics designed from *Alpha Phonics*. There are no flashy graphics, but it covers phonics and spelling well. The student can work independently.

| *English Skill:* **Remedial Reading** | *Grade:* **9-12*** | *Prerequisite:* **none** |

*The earlier remediation begins, the better.

Phonics Intervention, Saxon

▶ Teacher helps: teacher's manual, classroom materials kit

▶ Description: *Phonics Intervention* is designed for the older student who has reading and spelling difficulty. The student workbook serves as both a reference and practice book. The teacher's manual provides model dialogue, lesson plans, and supplementary materials. A classroom material kit contains card decks reviewing learned skills.

| *English Skill:* **Remedial Reading** | *Grade:* **9-12*** | *Prerequisite:* **none** |

*The earlier remediation begins, the better.

Developing Better Reading, Rod and Staff

▶ Teacher helps: teacher's manual

▶ Description: *Developing Better Reading* is an inexpensive workbook presenting a review of basic phonics, spelling, and syllabication rules for the remedial reading student.

| *English Skill:* **Literary Interpretation** | *Grade:* **9-12** | *Prerequisite:* **none** |

novel with worksheets, Progeny Press

▶ Teacher helps: answers included with worksheets

▶ Description: Those who enjoy a living book approach will appreciate the Progeny Press study guides for literature. The study guides are loose-leaf, ready for insertion into a three ring binder. Twenty guides are presently available for high school studies. Questions reflect a Christian worldview, so that even controversial novels can be discussed profitably. A synopsis of the novel, vocabulary activities, composition suggestions, basic reading comprehension, and more advanced critical thinking questions are all included.

English Skill: **Literary Interpretation**   *Grade:* **9**   *Prerequisite:* **none**

Fundamentals of Literature, Bob Jones University Press

▸ Teacher helps: teacher's edition, *Testbuilder* software

▸ Description: Analyzes various reading selections for the following elements: conflict, character, theme, structure, point of view, and moral tone. The student text includes introductory text for each selection, author biographies, and thought and discussion questions. *Cyrano de Bergerac* is studied in full. The teacher's edition contains the student pages, with additional helpful information for guiding discussion. Answers to the questions in the student text are also included. The *Testbuilder* software provides a testbank for customizing tests.

English Skill: **Literary Interpretation**   *Grade:* **10**   *Prerequisite:* **none**

Elements of Literature, Bob Jones University Press

▸ Teacher helps: teacher's edition, *Testbuilder* software

▸ Description: This text moves into advanced literary concepts with a study on different genres. The Shakespearean play *Romeo and Juliet* is studied in full. The teacher's edition has the same helpful features of the previous book. The *Testbuilder* software provides a testbank for customizing tests.

English Skill: **American Literature**   *Grade:* **7-12**   *Prerequisite:* **none**

American Literature, Alpha Omega

▸ Teacher helps: teacher's manual

▸ Description: This one semester chronological American literature course can be used as a supplement to the Alpha Omega *Language Arts* lifepacs or any other English program you are using. The same lifepac approach to learning described on page 36 is used in this course. Its adaptability to grades seven to twelve means it will be less rigorous than some choices.

English Skill: **American Literature**   *Grade:* **9-12**   *Prerequisite:* **none**

novels, two anthologies

▸ Teacher helps: *The Gold Book: American Literature*, Common Sense Press

▸ Description: *The Gold Book: American Literature* is part of the *Learning Language Arts Through Literature* series. It is organized by genres rather than chronologically. Genres studied include: the short story, the novel, and poetry. Three essay assignments; expository, descriptive, and narrative, are also included. Student will need to purchase the recommended novels and anthologies. Unlike other LLATL titles, this level has a teacher's book only.

English Skill: **American Literature**   *Grade:* **11**   *Prerequisite:* **none**

American Literature, Bob Jones University Press

▸ Teacher helps: teacher's edition, *Testbuilder* software

▸ Description: This text takes a chronological walk through American literature. Introductions explaining each major time period are accompanied by a time line. Biographical information on the various authors precedes the selections. Using this book in conjunction with American history makes it doubly effective. The two-part teacher edition contains full-sized student pages and plenty of help for preparing an excellent college preparatory course. The *Testbuilder* software provides a testbank for customizing tests.

English Skill: **British Literature**   *Grade:* **7-12**   *Prerequisite:* **none**

British Literature, Alpha Omega

▸ Teacher helps: teacher's manual

▸ Description: This one semester chronological British literature course can be used as a supplement to the Alpha Omega *Language Arts* lifepacs or any other English program you are using. The same lifepac approach to learning described on page 36 is used in this course. Its adaptability to grades seven to twelve means it will be less rigorous than some choices.

Reading & Literature (Cont'd)

English Skill: **British Literature**   *Grade:* **9-12**   *Prerequisite:* **none**

five novels, one anthology
- Teacher helps: *The Gold Book: British Literature,* Common Sense Press
- Description: *The Gold Book: British Literature* is the newest addition to the *Learning Language Arts Through Literature* series. Books studied include: *Frankenstein, Emma, A Tale of Two Cities, The Time Machine,* and *Animal Farm. The Mentor Book of Major British Poets* is also used. Composition requirements are included.

English Skill: **British Literature**   *Grade:* **12**   *Prerequisite:* **none**

British Literature, Bob Jones University Press
- Teacher helps: teacher's edition, *Testbuilder* software
- Description: This text takes a chronological walk through British literature. Introductions explaining each major time period are accompanied by a time line. Biographical information on the various authors precedes the selections. The two-part teacher edition contains full-sized student pages and plenty of help for preparing an excellent college preparatory course. The *Testbuilder* software provides a testbank for customizing tests. This text is a personal favorite of mine.

English Skill: **Ancient Literature**   *Grade:* **12**   *Prerequisite:* ******

**concurrent with ancient world history
Heroes of the City of Man, Peter Leithart, Canon Press
- Teacher helps: none
- Description: Peter Leithart analyzes the ancient pagan classics; The Iliad, The Odyssey, and The Aeneid from a Christian worldview. Thought-provoking questions conclude each section. *Heroes* is a valuable introduction for the Christian student who may cover this material again (from a vastly different viewpoint) in a secular college course.

English Skill: **Shakespeare**   *Grade:* **11-12**   *Prerequisite:* ******

**after or concurrent with British literature
Brightest Heaven of Invention, Peter Leithart, Canon Press
- Teacher helps: none
- Description: Another Peter Leithart book which this time walks the student through six of Shakespeare's plays. Two historical plays, two tragedies, and two comedies are included. *Brightest Heaven of Invention* is an in-depth study from a Christian worldview.

English Skill: **Spenser**   *Grade:* **11-12**   *Prerequisite:* ******

**after or concurrent with British literature
Fierce Wars and Faithful Loves, Roy Maynard, Canon Press
- Teacher helps: teacher's manual
- Description: For the motivated student of English literature, Roy Maynard has updated and annotated Book One of *The Faerie Queene* by Edmund Spenser. Maynard's Christian worldview is evident in his commentary. "Sword Talk" at the end of each chapter provides a vocabulary list and questions.

English Skill: **Literary Genres**   *Grade:* **9-12**   *Prerequisite:* **none**

Reading Between the Lines, Gene Edward Veith, Crossway
▸ Teacher helps: teacher's manual
▸ Description: *Reading Between the Lines* is an excellent introduction to both the forms and history of literature. A literary history course could be designed using *Reading Between the Lines* as a guide to choosing selections from different literary genres or time periods.

English Skill: **Critical Reading**   *Grade:* **9-12**   *Prerequisite:* **none**

How to Read a Book, Mortimer Adler, Simon & Schuster
▸ Teacher helps: none
▸ Description: *How to Read a Book* is subtitled *The Classic Guide to Intelligent Reading*. A well-respected guide for over 60 years, it teaches the reader to actively and intelligently interact with his reading material. Different levels and techniques of reading are taught which can be employed when reading various types of books. This book would be especially helpful for any college bound student.

A Note on Poetry

No study of literature would be complete without attention to the beauty of poetry. Many sources are available. Student literature textbooks will usually contain a liberal sprinkling of poetry. This is especially helpful when the poetry is placed in historical context, as in American, British, and world literature texts.

Paperback poetry collections are also available. *The Harp and Laurel Wreath: Poetry and Dictation for the Classical Curriculum* by Laura Berquist contains both poetry and prose dictation or recitation selections for all ages, arranged by grade level. Study questions follow selections for older students, with answers in the back of the book. Poetry collections such as *The Mentor Book of American Poetry (also Major British Poets)* or Dover Publications thrift editions, available through many bookstores, provide inexpensive means for providing poetry studies for your home school. Two lists follow of well-recognized American and British poets. Although certainly not exhaustive, it gives you some place to start.

American poets: Anne Bradstreet, William Cullen Bryant, Henry Wadsworth Longfellow, John Greenleaf Whittier, James Russell Lowell, Oliver Wendall Holmes, Walt Whitman, Sidney Lanier, Emily Dickinson, Robert Frost, Edna St. Vincent Millay, Carl Sandburg, e.e. cummings, and T.S. Eliot.

British poets: Edmund Spenser, William Shakespeare, John Donne, George Herbert, John Milton, Isaac Watts, Robert Burns, William Blake, William Wordsworth, Samuel Coleridge, Percy Bysshe Shelley, John Keats, Lord Tennyson, Robert Browning, and Christina Rossetti.

AMERICAN LITERATURE

This list of suggested high school literature is by no means a complete list. There are many other excellent books worth reading that are not listed here. When a study guide is available for a book, this is listed after the author.

Title	Author	Guides
The Adventures of Huckleberry Finn	Mark Twain	Progeny Press
The Adventures of Tom Sawyer	Mark Twain	Progeny Press
Billy Budd, Moby Dick	Herman Melville	
The Call of the Wild	Jack London	
The Deerslayer, The Last of the Mohicans	James Fenimore Cooper	
The Great Gatsby	F. Scott Fitzgerald	Progeny Press
The Good Earth	Pearl Buck	
Great American Short Stories	Dell Publishing	LLATL's *The Gold Book: American Literature*
Heart of Darkness	Joseph Conrad	Progeny Press
The Song of Hiawatha, Evangeline	Henry Wadsworth Longfellow	
The House of Seven Gables	Nathaniel Hawthorne	
In His Steps	Charles Sheldon	A-O *Language Arts 1009*
The Incredible Journey	S. Burnford	
The Island of the Blue Dolphin	Scott O'Dell	Progeny Press
Little Women	Louisa May Alcott	
The Mentor Book of American Poetry	Oscar Williams	LLATL's *The Gold Book: American Literature*
The Merry Adventures of Robin Hood	Howard Pyle	
The Miracle Worker	William Gibson	A-O *Language Arts 908*
My Antonia	Willa Cather	
The Old Man and the Sea	Ernest Hemingway	A-O *Language Arts 1108*, LLATL's *The Gold Book: American Literature*
Our Town	Thornton Wilder	A-O *Language Arts 1107*
The Pearl	John Steinbeck	LLATL's *The Gold Book: American Literature*
The Scarlet Letter	Nathaniel Hawthorne	Progeny Press
The Yearling	Majorie Rawlings	Progeny Press

BRITISH LITERATURE

This list of suggested high school literature is by no means a complete list. There are many other excellent books worth reading that are not listed here. When a Christian study help is available for a book, this is listed after the author.

Title	Author	Guides
Adv. of Sherlock Holmes	Sir Conan Doyle	
Alice's Adventures in Wonderland	Lewis Carroll	
Through the Looking Glass	Lewis Carroll	
Animal Farm	George Orwell	*LLATL's The Gold Book: British Literature*
1984	George Orwell	
Anne of Green Gables	Lucy Maude Montgomery	
As You Like It	William Shakespeare	
A Tale of Two Cities	Charles Dickens	*LLATL's The Gold Book: British Literature*
Best of Father Brown	G.K. Chesterton	
Best of James Herriot	James Herriot	
The Black Arrow	Robert Louis Stevenson	
Captains Courageous	Rudyard Kipling	
The Canterbury Tales	Geoffrey Chaucer	
David Copperfield	Charles Dickens	
Emma	Jane Austen	*LLATL's The Gold Book: British Literature*
The Faerie Queene	Edmund Spenser	*Fierce Wars and Faithful Loves*
Frankenstein	Mary Shelley	*LLATL's The Gold Book: British Literature*
Gray Wolf	George MacDonald	
Great Expectations	Charles Dickens	
Gulliver's Travels	Jonathan Swift	
Hamlet	William Shakespeare	A-O *Language Arts 1206,* Progeny Press, *Brightest Heaven of Invention*
Henry V	William Shakespeare	*Brightest Heaven of Invention*
The High King	Lloyd Alexander	
The Hobbit	J.R.R. Tolkein	Progeny Press
The Hound of the Baskervilles	Sir Conan Doyle	
Ivanhoe, The Talisman, and/or other titles	Sir Walter Scott	
Jane Eyre	Charlotte Bronte	Progeny Press
Julius Caesar	William Shakespeare	*Brightest Heaven of Invention*

BRITISH LITERATURE (continued)

Title	Author	Guides
Kidnapped	Robert Louis Stevenson	
Kim	Rudyard Kipling	
The Lord of the Rings	J.R.R. Tolkien	
Macbeth	William Shakespeare	*Brightest Heaven of Invention*
Merchant of Venice	William Shakespeare	Progeny Press
Much Ado about Nothing	William Shakespeare	*Brightest Heaven of Invention*
Oliver Twist	Charles Dickens	
Paradise Lost	John Milton	
Perelandra *Out of the Silent Planet* *That Hideous Strength*	C.S. Lewis	Progeny Press (for *Perelandra* and *Out of the Silent Planet* only)
Pilgrim's Progress	John Bunyan	
Pride and Prejudice	Jane Austen	
Pygmalion	George Bernard Shaw	
Robinson Crusoe	Daniel DeFoe	
Romeo and Juliet	William Shakespeare	Progeny Press
Sir Gawain and the Green Knight	J.R.R. Tolkien version	
The Strange Case of Dr. Jekyll and Mr. Hyde	Robert Lewis Stevenson	Progeny Press
A Tale of Two Cities	Charles Dickens	Progeny Press
Tales from Shakespeare	Charles and Mary Lamb	
Taming of the Shrew	William Shakespeare	*Brightest Heaven of Invention*
The Time Machine	H.G. Wells	*LLATL's The Gold Book: British Literature*
Treasure Island	Robert Louis Stevenson	
Wuthering Heights	Emily Bronte	

WORLD LITERATURE

This list of suggested high school literature is by no means a complete list. There are many other excellent books worth reading that are not listed here. When a Christian study guide is available for a book, this is listed after the author.

Title	Author	Guides
The Aeneid	Virgil	Heroes of the City of Man
Anna Karenina	Leo Tolstoy	
Arabian Nights	Andrew Lang	
Around the World in Eighty Days	Jules Verne	
The Brothers Karamazov	Fyodor Dostoevsky	
Crime and Punishment	Fyodor Dostoevsky	
Cry, the Beloved Country	Alan Paton	
Cyrano de Bergerac	Edmond Rostand	
Don Quixote	Miguel de Cervantes	
The Iliad	Homer	Heroes of the City of Man
The Odyssey	Homer	Heroes of the City of Man
Hunchback of Notre Dame	Victor Hugo	
Kon Tiki	Thor Heyerdahl	
Les Miserables	Victor Hugo	
Quo Vadis	Henry Sienkiewicz	
Swiss Family Robinson	Johann Wyss	
Twenty Thousand Leagues under the Sea	Jules Verne	A-O Language Arts 909
War and Peace	Leo Tolstoy	

STANDARD
ENGLISH COURSE EXAMPLES

| *Course:* **English I** | *Grade:* **9** | *Prerequisite:* **none** |

Text

Writing and Grammar, Bob Jones University Press
Format Writing, Wordsmith
Wordly Wise 3000 #6, Educator's Publishing Service
selected novels with worksheets, Progeny Press

Teacher helps

teacher's edition
included in text
answer key
answer key included with worksheets

▸ Description: This is a standard English I course. A combination of grammar, mechanics, composition, vocabulary, and literature may be studied at this level. BJUP's *Writing and Grammar* worktext covers writing and grammar. For additional writing activities use *Format Writing's* first section, "Single Paragraph Formats." Vocabulary can be studied using *Wordly Wise 3000 #6*. Read at least two novels, writing a book report on each. These can be chosen to coincide with the topic being studied in history if desired. See the various literature lists for guide availability.

| *Course:* **English II** | *Grade:* **10** | *Prerequisite:* **English I** |

Text

Writing and Grammar, Bob Jones University Press
Format Writing, Wordsmith
Wordly Wise 3000 #7, Educator's Publishing Service
Reading between the Lines, Gene Veith/Crossway Books
or **selected novels with worksheets**, Progeny Press

Teacher helps

teacher's edition
included in text
answer key
no guide available
answer key included with worksheets

▸ Description: This is a standard English II course. Composition, vocabulary, and literature are studied. If additional grammar work is desired, the student can continue in BJUP's *Writing and Grammar* worktexts. For composition continue with *Format Writing* doing "Section Two, Five Paragraph Essays: Elements and Formats." Vocabulary work continues with *Wordly Wise 3000 #7*. For literature use *Reading between the Lines*. This is a challenging but readable book on how Christians should respond to literature. I highly recommend it. Grading can include discussion along with chapter and book summaries. If you feel this book is too challenging for your teen, consider having him read at least 2-4 novels using literature guides.

| *Course:* **English III** | *Grade:* **11** | *Prerequisite:* **English II** |

Text

Format Writing, Wordsmith
Wordly Wise 3000 #8, Educator's Publishing Service
American Literature, Bob Jones University Press

Teacher helps

included in text
answer key
teacher's guide, testbank

▸ Description: This is a standard English III course. A combination of composition, vocabulary, and American literature may be studied. For composition continue with *Format Writing*, doing "Sections Three and Four: The Principle of Condensation and Major Papers." Include practice in skills presented in these sections and one major paper. Vocabulary continues with *Wordly Wise 3000 #8*. For literature use the excellent anthology from Bob Jones University Press.

Course: **English IV**	*Grade:* **12**	*Prerequisite:* **English III**

Text	**Teacher helps**
Format Writing, Wordsmith	included in text
Wordly Wise 3000 #9, Educator's Publishing Service	answer key
British Literature, Bob Jones University Press	teacher's guide, testbank

▸ Description: This is a standard English IV course. A combination of composition, vocabulary, and literature may be studied. For composition continue working with skills learned in "Sections Three and Four" of *Format Writing*. Include a minimum of one major paper per semester. Vocabulary continues with *Wordly Wise 3000 #9*. For literature use the excellent anthology from Bob Jones University Press.

ADVANCED
ENGLISH COURSE EXAMPLES

Course: **English I Advanced**	*Grade:* **9**	*Prerequisite:* **none**

Text	**Teacher helps**
Jensen's Grammar 1-3, Wordsmith	included in text
Jensen's Punctuation, Wordsmith	included in text
Format Writing, Wordsmith	included in text
Latin I or Greek I, Wordsmith	included in text
selected novels with worksheets, Progeny Press	answer key included with worksheets

▸ Description: In advanced English I the pace is accelerated with more required of the student. Use *Jensen's Grammar 1-3* for the grammar study. Begin *Jensen's Punctuation* after completing *Jensen's Grammar, Book Two*. For composition use *Format Writing*, but do both "Section One" and "Section Two" and its accompanying writing. For vocabulary use *Latin I or Greek I*. Consider reading two novels a semester followed by a book report on each, or use a literature guide. See the various literature lists for guide availability. Novels can be chosen to coincide with the topic studied in history, if desired.

Course: **English II Advanced**	*Grade:* 10	*Prerequisite:* **English I Advanced**

Text	**Teacher helps**
Jensen's Punctuation, Wordsmith	included in text
Format Writing, Wordsmith	included in text
Latin I, II or Greek I, Wordsmith	included in text
Reading between the Lines, Gene Veith/Crossway Books	no guide available
selected novels with worksheets, Progeny Press	answer key included with worksheets

▸ Description: In advanced English II the pace is accelerated, requiring more of the student. Complete Jensen's Punctuation. For composition continue with *Format Writing* doing "Sections Three and Four." Do "Section Three" exercises first semester and "Section Four" with a major paper second semester. Vocabulary work continues with *Latin I, II,* or *Greek I*. For literature use *Reading between the Lines*. This is a challenging but readable book on how Christians should respond to literature. I highly recommend it. Grading can include discussion along with chapter and book summaries. Consider studying *Reading between the Lines* first semester and two novels the second semester. See the various literature lists for guide availability.

Advanced English Course Examples (cont'd)

Course: **English III Advanced**	Grade: **11**	Prerequisite: **English II Advanced**

Text

	Teacher helps
Format Writing, Wordsmith	included in text
Latin I, II or Greek I, Wordsmith	included in text
American Literature, Bob Jones University Press	teacher's guide, testbank

▶ Description: In advanced English III the pace is accelerated, requiring more of the student. For composition, review *Format Writing*, "Sections Three and Four." Continue to use the condensation and summarization skills learned. Write one major paper per semester. Vocabulary continues with *Latin I, II or Greek I*. For literature use the excellent anthology from Bob Jones University Press.

Course: **English IV Advanced**	Grade: **12**	Prerequisite: **English III Advanced**

Text

	Teacher helps
Format Writing, Wordsmith	included in text
Latin I, II or Greek I, Wordsmith	included in text
British Literature, Bob Jones University Press	teacher's guide, testbank

▶ Description: In advanced English IV the pace is accelerated, requiring more of the student. For composition continue with the skills learned in *Format Writing*. Require a minimum of two major papers per semester. Continue vocabulary with *Latin I, II or Greek I* if not already completed. If finished consider adding *Wordly Wise 3000 #9*. For literature use the excellent anthology from Bob Jones Univerity Press.

> ### A Note on Bob Jones University Press
> ### TestBuilder Software
>
> If you are planning to use several Bob Jones University Press textbooks during the course of your student's high school program, you may be interested in their *Testbuilder* software. *Testbuilder* allows you to select a wide variety of test questions, add your own questions, and print out both a copy of the test and the key.
>
> Presently high school histories and literatures, ninth grade grammar, life science, earth science, biology, family living, and health are available. Download privileges are included for other subjects as they become available.

MATHEMATICS COURSES

Many of us feel inadequate when it comes to higher level math. If struggles arise, you might:

1. learn along with your student.
2. hire a tutor for your teen (maybe an older home schooled student).
3. stretch an advanced math text over an extra semester or year.
4. look for or start a cooperative class for home schooled students.
5. look into the availability of junior or community college math courses.

Suggestions for mathematics courses begin on the next page. These suggestions represent publishers widely available on the home school retail or catalog market. Math U See, a popular home school product sold through distributors, is also included. For a wider look at mathematics products and a more complete look at the products mentioned here, I once again point you to Cathy Duffy and Mary Pride's helpful curriculum guides.

The chart below lists popular home school math publishers and special features which enhance their methodology. If one of these products looks appealing, see what Cathy Duffy or Mary Pride has to say.

High School Math Publishers	Textbook	Worktext	Videos	Manipulatives	Satellite	Software
A Beka Books	X		X			
Alpha Omega		X			X	
Bob Jones University Press	X			X		
Chalkdust Company	X		X			
Cornerstone Curriculum Project	X		X			
Harold Jacobs (W.H. Freeman)	X					
Key Curriculum Press		X				
Math U See	X		X	X		
Saxon	X		X*			
School of Tomorrow		X	X			
The Teaching Company			X			
Videotext		X	X			
*videos for use with Saxon are available from Teaching Tape Technology (see Mary Pride).						

MATHEMATICS

Course: Remedial Math   Grade: **9-12***   Prerequisite: **none**

*The earlier remediation begins, the better.
Calculadder 1-6, Providence Project
▸ Teacher helps: keys included with workbook
▸ Description: *Calculadder* is a series of workbooks drilling basic math facts and skills with the goal of building speed in every math process. *Level One* begins with basic addition and subtraction. *Level Six* finishes with fractions, unit conversions, and pre-geometry. This is not a stand-alone program but would supplement your main math program.

Course: Remedial Math   Grade: **9-12***   Prerequisite: **none**

*The earlier remediation begins, the better.
Keys to Fractions, Key Curriculum Press
Keys to Decimals, Key Curriculum Press
Keys to Percents, Key Curriculum Press
▸ Teacher helps: separate answer keys & tests
▸ Description: Each of these workbook sets review basic skills starting at the beginning of the concept and increasing slowly in difficulty.

Course: Consumer Math   Grade: **9-12**   Prerequisite: **none**

Consumer Math, Bob Jones University Press
Student Activities Book, Bob Jones University Press
▸ Teacher helps: teacher's guide, tests & key, teacher's edition for student activities book
▸ Description: A course teaching the mathematics needed for daily living.

Course: Algebra I   Grade: **9-12**   Prerequisite: **Pre-Algebra**

Keys to Algebra, Key Curriculum Press
▸ Teacher helps: separate answer keys & tests
▸ Description: A slower, workbook approach which introduces one concept at a time. This program is a good precursor to a more in-depth algebra I. It may be sufficient for junior college entrance for the student who struggles with math, but the course will probably not contain enough content for the student whose SAT scores are important.

Course: Algebra & Geometry   Grade: **9-12**   Prerequisite: **Pre-Algebra**

Basic Algebra & Geometry, Math U See
▸ Teacher helps: teacher's manual, videos, math manipulatives
▸ Description: Math U See is a full-line math curriculum available for all grade levels. The videos explain mathematical concepts through the use of appropriate math manipulatives. Although the videos are designed for teacher use, students may enjoy watching them with the parent. The teacher then presents the lesson to the student, with the student finishing the lesson by working independently on workbook problems. This product is currently available only through distributors. See Appendix A for address information.

Course: Algebra I   *Grade:* **9**   *Prerequisite:* **Pre-Algebra**

Alpha Omega Lifepacs 901-910, Alpha Omega
▸ Teacher helps: teacher's edition
▸ Description: Ten worktexts walk your student through algebra I. The teacher guide works out solutions step-by-step. Some students may find the smaller individual worktexts less intimidating than a large textbook. This is also available in the computerized *Switched on Schoolhouse* format.

Course: Algebra I   *Grade:* **9**   *Prerequisite:* **Pre-Algebra**

Algebra I, Bob Jones University Press
Algebra I Student Activities Book, Bob Jones University Press
▸ Teacher helps: teacher's edition, tests and key, teacher's edition for student activity book
▸ Description: This newly revised algebra I text emphasizes understanding of mathematical concepts. Solutions are contained in the teacher's edition. The activity book contains both remediation and enrichment activities. This course can be studied via satellite through BJU's HomeSat. It would be a fine college preparatory choice.

Course: Algebra I   *Grade:* **9**   *Prerequisite:* **Pre-Algebra**

Algebra I, Saxon
Algebra I Solutions Manual, Saxon
▸ Teacher helps: answers and tests included in home school kit
▸ Description: A thorough algebra I course which also incorporates beginning geometry. If the student has mastered all basic mathematical operations, calculator use can be introduced when using this text.

Course: Remedial Geometry   *Grade:* **9-12**   *Prerequisite:* **none**

Keys to Geometry, Key Curriculum Press
▸ Teacher helps: separate keys
▸ Description: A slower paced workbook approach to geometry which provides a simple introduction to geometric constructions and terminology. Supplementation will be necessary for college preparation, or use it as an introduction to a more thorough geometry program.

Course: Geometry   *Grade:* **10**   *Prerequisite:* **Algebra I**

Geometry paces, School of Tomorrow
▸ Teacher helps: teacher's manual, videos
▸ Description: This is a complete geometry course with practice in geometric proofs. The videos provide a very helpful enhancement to this worktext approach.

Course: Geometry   *Grade:* **10**   *Prerequisite:* **Algebra I**

Geometry, Bob Jones University Press
Geometry Student Activities Book, Bob Jones University Press
▸ Teacher helps: teacher's manual, tests and key, teacher's edition to student activities book
▸ Description: Unlike Saxon, Bob Jones geometry is offered in a separate textbook. This is especially helpful for the student whose high school plan does not include four years of mathematics. A study of proofs, theorems, and real-life geometry are included. The activity book contains both remediation and enrichment activities. This course is fine college preparatory material. It is available via satellite through BJU's HomeSat.

Mathematics (cont'd)

| *Course:* **Algebra II** | *Grade:* **10-12** | *Prerequisite:* **Alg I & Geometry** |

Algebra II, Math U See
▸ Teacher helps: teacher's manual, videos
▸ Description: *Algebra II* continues to use videos to introduce teachers to mathematical concepts, although the use of manipulatives is discontinued at this level. Teachers then introduce concepts to students. Students follow-up with workbook problems. Many students will find Math U See's approach friendlier and less intense than other programs. This product is currently available only through distributors. See Appendix A for address information.

| *Course:* **Algebra II** | *Grade:* **11** | *Prerequisite:* **Algebra I** |

Algebra II, *2nd Edition*, Bob Jones University Press
Algebra II Student Activities Book, Bob Jones University Press
▸ Teacher helps: teacher's manual, tests and key, teacher's edition for student activities book
▸ Description: Newly revised, *Algebra II* reviews and extends the learning presented in *Algebra I*. Solutions are contained in the teacher's edition. The activity book contains both remediation and enrichment activities. For the mathematically challenged parent, this course can be studied via satellite through BJU's HomeSat.

| *Course:* **Algebra II** | *Grade:* **10** | *Prerequisite:* **Algebra I** |

Algebra II, Saxon
Algebra II Solutions Manual, Saxon
▸ Teacher helps: answers and tests included in home school kit
▸ Description: A thorough algebra II course which continues incorporating geometry. Math problems at this level often having multiple steps requiring extensive computation. If answers are rounded before the final step they will not match the answer key. For this reason consider using a calculator with this text.

| *Course:* **Trigonometry** | *Grade:* **11-12** | *Prerequisite:* **Alg. I & II, Geom.** |

Trigonometry, Math U See
▸ Teacher helps: teacher's manual, videos
▸ Description: The Math U See program is now available in trigonometry. Video instruction for the teacher continues but manipulatives are no longer used. This product is currently available only through distributors. See Appendix A for address information.

| *Course:* **Advanced Math** | *Grade:* **12** | *Prerequisite:* **Algebra II** |

Advanced Math, Bob Jones University Press
▸ Teacher helps: teacher's manual, no separate solutions manual
▸ Description: Course includes a continuation of algebraic principles, trigonometry, and an introduction to calculus. Unless math is your strength, consider using BJU's HomeSat for this course. (We left it to the junior college!)

Course: **Advanced Math**   *Grade:* **11-12**   *Prerequisite:* **Algebra II**

Advanced Mathematics, Saxon
Advanced Mathematics Solutions Manual, Saxon
▸ Teacher helps: answers and tests included in home school kit
▸ Description: A very challenging precalculus course which includes one half year of plane geometry. This book can be taken over the course of 2-4 semesters. Calculator use is recommended, and the graphing calculator is introduced.

Course: **Calculus**   *Grade:* **12**   *Prerequisite:* **Advanced Math**

Calculus, Saxon
Calculus Solutions Manual, Saxon
▸ Teacher helps: answers and tests included in home school kit
▸ Description: This course is equivalent to two semesters of college calculus. If successfully completed, the student is ready to take the College Board's Advanced Placement exam in Calculus.

Course: **Accounting**   *Grade:* **7-12**   *Prerequisite:* **none**

Accounting, Alpha Omega
▸ Teacher helps: teacher's guide
▸ Description: Accounting is a new lifepac program available for the first time in 2000. Consider it a math or business elective.

Geometry and the PSAT

Students will perform better on the PSAT if they have studied geometry prior to taking the test. This is an important consideration when choosing a math series.

Saxon math does not have a separate geometry text, making it necessary to go through *Algebra I*, *Algebra II* and *Advanced Math* to get a full year of geometry. This means geometry will not be completed before taking the PSAT. An option is to skip *Math 87* and begin *Algebra I* in eighth grade, thus speeding the progression through the books. However, consider the ability level of the student before making this jump.

If you prefer a series with a separate geometry text, consider the series from Bob Jones University Press. We regularly hear very positive reports from customers using this series. If you would like to try a computerized program, Alpha Omega's *Switched On Schoolhouse's* tenth grade math won the 2000 Practical Homeschooling Software Reader Awards for best geometry software. (The other math courses in *Switched on Schoolhouse* have been similarly awarded.)

SCIENCE COURSES

My high school memories of biology are positive. My memories of chemistry are entirely different. My chief recollection is of two girlfriends and myself holding back tears and sniffing our way through yet another test we did not understand. I passed chemistry, not on merit, but on the kindness of a merciful teacher. The grief of chemistry motivated me to persuade my counselor *not* to include physics in my next year's studies. If your memories are similar, take courage. There is hope! Thanks to satellite technology and videos, options for teaching these difficult courses at home are increasing.

In the previous section on math, I began mentioning Bob Jones University's HomeSat. With the purchase of a small satellite dish and a reasonable monthly fee, HomeSat allows you to record any course offered through its satellite service. The offerings include elementary and high school level classes, with the difficult high school courses (math, science, and foreign language) available. For the student headed into the sciences at the college level this would be an excellent choice. All HomeSat courses use Bob Jones University Press textbooks.

School of Tomorrow offers video courses including the high school sciences. We have personally used their biology and physical science videos and have been very pleased with the interesting presentation and high production level. (Watching the physical science videos, I was truly amazed that they could make it interesting to *me*!) Addresses for both Bob Jones University Press and School of Tomorrow are in Appendix A.

Another strategy for teaching science lab courses is for the student to apply for early admissions at his local junior college. Courses that are difficult to teach at home can be taken at the junior college for both high school and college credit. Check with your local junior or community college for requirements and information.

Following are some suggested courses. Again, my goal is not to make an exhaustive list, but to include some of the easiest to use or most widely available materials on the home school market. There are other academically sound products available.

Science Courses

Course: Remedial Science Grade: 9-12 Prerequisite: none

The Wonders of Science, 6 book series, Steck Vaughn
▸ Teacher helps: teacher's edition with answers
▸ Description: These science books are offered for the student who is reading significantly below grade level. They contain core content for both biology and general science courses at an easier reading level. These texts are published by a secular company but are largely non-offensive to a Christian worldview.

Course: Physical Science Grade: 10 Prerequisite: Algebra I

Physical Science worktexts, School of Tomorrow
▸ Teacher helps: answer keys/videos
▸ Description: This physical science course is an introduction to both chemistry and physics. It could probably serve as one of the lab sciences for the non-science bound student without taking a full year of chemistry or physics. It also provides a good introduction for the student who does plan to include both chemistry and physics in his high school program. An interesting and professional video presentation makes these worktexts a good choice. Although the course can be done with worktext only, the videos greatly enhance the course. The course teaches itself and is easy to grade.

Course: Physical Science Grade: 9 Prerequisite: none

The Physical World, Bob Jones University Press
Student Lab Manual, Bob Jones University Press
▸ Teacher helps: teacher's edition, tests and answer key, teacher's edition for student lab manual
▸ Description: This new text is an introduction to chemistry and physics. Some parents teach this course using the textbook, answering textbook questions (answers in the teacher's manual), and taking tests. Using the student laboratory manual adds to the thoroughness of the course. Extensive use of the lab manual would make this a good college preparatory lab course. This course is available on BJU's HomeSat.

Course: Physical Science Grade: 8-9 Prerequisite: none

Exploring Creation with Physical Science, Dr. Jay Wiles, Apologia
▸ Teacher helps: solutions and test book
▸ Descriptions: Although Apologia's textbooks do not have the color and flash of some other choices, they do have a conversational writing style. This means information is not so densely packed and therefore easier for some students to grasp. Instructions for lab work are contained in the student text. This book is intended for eighth graders with a strong science background or ninth graders with weaker science backgrounds. See www.highschoolscience.com for information on on-line courses.

Course: Life Science Grade: 7-12 Prerequisite: none

Life Science Lifepac Select, Alpha Omega
▸ Teacher helps: teacher's guide
▸ Description: Alpha Omega *Select* electives are lifepacs topically chosen to create a one semester course. Since the *Lifepac Select* courses include both junior high and high school level lifepacs, this course will be less challenging than some other choices.

Course: **Biology**	*Grade:* **9**	*Prerequisite:* **none**

Biology worktexts, School of Tomorrow
▸ Teacher helps: answer keys/videos
▸ Description: An interesting and professional video presentation makes these worktexts a good choice. Although the course can be done with worktext only, the videos greatly enhance the course. The course teaches itself and is easy to grade.

Course: **Biology**	*Grade:* **9-10**	*Prerequisite:* **none**

Life Science, Bob Jones University Press
Student Activities Book, Bob Jones University Press
▸ Teacher helps: teacher's edition, tests and answer key, teacher's edition for student activity book
▸ Description: For the student needing an easier text, this middle school life science text is a good possibility. Consider using it for the student not heading into the sciences. Name the course "biology" on the transcript. A student activities book offers the hands-on activities necessary for a lab science. The biology dissection kit and video, also available from BJUP, can be successfully used with the text. *Life Science* is available on HomeSat.

Course: **Biology**	*Grade:* **10**	*Prerequisite:* **none**

Biology, Bob Jones University Press
Biology Lab Manual, Bob Jones University Press
dissection kit & video, Bob Jones University Press
▸ Teacher helps: teacher's edition, tests and answer key, teacher's edition of lab manual, lab manual supplement for home educators, *Testbuilder* software
▸ Description: This challenging course will give any student headed into the sciences an excellent background. A lab manual with activities reinforcing textbook concepts is available. In addition, a reasonably priced dissection kit (complete with specimens) provides all you need to do dissection at home. A dissection video is also available. This course is available through BJU's HomeSat program.

Course: **Biology**	*Grade:* **9-10**	*Prerequisite:* **

**take concurrently with Algebra I
Exploring Creation with Biology, Dr. Jay Wiles, Apologia
▸ Teacher helps: solutions and test book, available on CD-ROM
▸ Description: Although Apologia's textbooks do not have the color and flash of some other choices, they do have a conversational writing style. This means information is not so densely packed and therefore easier for some students to grasp. Instructions for lab work are contained in the student text. Dr. Wile's book makes another fine choice for college preparation. See www.highschoolscience.com for information on on-line courses.

Course: **Advanced Biology**	*Grade:* **11-12**	*Prerequisite:* **

**Biology I and Chemistry I
The Human Body: Fearfully and Wonderfully Made, Dr. Jay Wiles, Apologia
▸ Teacher helps: solutions and test book
▸ Description: For those students on an accelerated science schedule, Apologia now has advanced biology available. This is equivalent to a first year college course. See Apologia's Web site, www.highschoolscience.com, for complete information.

SCIENCE COURSES (CONT'D)

Course: **Chemistry**	Grade: **11**	Prerequisite: **

**Algebra I, Biology, Physical Science
Chemistry worktexts, School of Tomorrow

▸ Teacher helps: answer keys/videos

▸ Description: It is my tendency to view every chemistry course as advanced. I have no personal experience with this course, but judging from our experience with other School of Tomorrow sciences, I assume its video presentation makes it more accessible than other chemistry courses. Although the course can be done with worktext only, if the video quality is as good as the other science courses we have used, they should greatly enhance the course.

Course: **Chemistry**	Grade: **11**	Prerequisite: **

**Algebra I (although more math is better.)
Chemistry, Bob Jones University Press
Chemistry Lab Manual, Bob Jones University Press

▸ Teacher helps: teacher's edition, tests and keys, teacher's edition for lab manual

▸ Description: This challenging course will give any student headed into the sciences an excellent background. This course is also available through BJU's HomeSat program.

Course: **Chemistry**	Grade: **10-11**	Prerequisite: **Algebra I**

Exploring Creation with Chemistry, Dr. Jay Wiles, Apologia

▸ Teacher helps: solutions and test book, available on CD-ROM

▸ Description: Another book from Apologia, with a more conversational style than your typical chemistry book. This is definitely a college preparatory course. See Cathy Duffy for a thorough review on this book. Also see www.highschoolscience.com for information on on-line courses.

Course: **Advanced Chemistry**	Grade: **11-12**	Prerequisite: **Alg. I & Chemistry I**

Advanced Chemistry in Creation, Dr. Jay Wiles, Apologia

▸ Teacher helps: solutions and test book

▸ Description: For those students on an accelerated science program, Apologia now has advanced chemistry available. This is equivalent to a first year college course. See Apologia's Web site, www.highschoolscience.com, for complete information.

Course: **Physics**	Grade: **12**	Prerequisite: **

**Algebra I, Physical Science
Physics worktexts, School of Tomorrow

▸ Teacher helps: answer keys/videos

▸ Description: Along with chemistry, I tend to view every physics course as advanced. I have no personal experience with this course, but judging from our experiences with other School of Tomorrow science videos, I assume it will be less difficult to understand than other physics courses. Although the course can be done with worktext only, if the video quality is as good as the other science courses we have used, they should greatly enhance the course.

Course: **Physics**	*Grade:* **12**	*Prerequisite:* **Algebra II**

Physics, Bob Jones University Press
Physics Lab Manual, Bob Jones University Press
▸ Teacher helps: teacher's edition, teacher's edition for student lab manual, lab manual supplement for home educators, testbank
▸ Description: This challenging course will provide the background needed for the young math and science scholar. If this one is way over your head consider the BJU HomeSat program.

Course: **Physics**	*Grade:* **12**	*Prerequisite:* **Algebra II**

Physics, Saxon
▸ Teacher helps: answer key and tests available in home school kit, solutions manual available separately
▸ Description: This is the last textbook in the Saxon series. Students completing this course successfully will be ready for the Advanced Placement physics exam and for majoring in college math and sciences.

Course: **Physics**	*Grade:* **11-12**	*Prerequisite:* **

**Algebra II* (Saxon) or 1 semester of trigonometry
Exploring Creation with Physics, Dr. Jay Wiles, Apologia
▸ Teacher helps: solutions and test book
▸ Description: Another college preparatory book for the serious science and mathematics student. See Cathy Duffy for a thorough review and www.highschoolscience.com for information on on-line courses.

Course: **Astronomy/Geology Elective**	*Grade:* **9-12**	*Prerequisite:* **none**

Earth Science, Bob Jones University Press
Earth Science Student Activities Book, Bob Jones University Press
▸ Teacher helps: teacher's edition, tests and answer key, teacher's edition for student activity book
▸ Description: For the student not heading into the sciences but needing a third science credit, consider this thorough middle school textbook. This course could serve as two one-semester courses: astronomy and geology. This course is available on HomeSat.

Course: **Geology Elective**	*Grade:* **7-12**	*Prerequisite:* **none**

Geology Lifepac Select, Alpha Omega
▸ Teacher helps: teacher's manual with answers
▸ Description: *Geology Lifepac Select* uses lifepacs chosen from Alpha Omega's junior high and high school level science courses. This makes the study less challenging and appropriate for the non-college bound or student not headed into the sciences. This is a half year course and would earn one half credit. You could pair it with the half credit *Astronomy Lifepac Select* for a full third year of science.

SCIENCE COURSES (CONT'D)

Course: **Astronomy Elective**   *Grade:* **7-12**   *Prerequisite:* **none**

Astronomy Lifepac Select, Alpha Omega
  ‣ Teacher helps: teacher's manual with answers
  ‣ Description: *Astronomy Lifepac Select* uses lifepacs chosen from Alpha Omega's junior high and high school level science courses. This makes the study less challenging and appropriate for the non-college bound or student not headed into the sciences. This is a half-year course and would earn one half credit. You could pair it with the half credit *Geology Lifepac Select* for a full third year of science.

Course: **Creation Science Elective**   *Grade:* **9-12**   *Prerequisite:* **none**

Darwin's Black Box, Michael Behe
Unlocking the Mysteries of Creation, Dennis Peterson
  ‣ Teacher helps: none available
  ‣ Description: *Darwin's Black Box* is a book supporting intelligent design of the universe. It is written from a Christian perspective and is very readable. (One of my students read this book after reading Darwin's *Origin of the Species*. He then wrote a comparison paper to finish the course.) *Unlocking the Mysteries of Creation* is a large format, heavily illustrated book with a question and answer format that explores many interesting facts. Many other living books on creation science can be found at Christian bookstores.

A Note on Math and Science

Something that has undoubtedly become clear as you have progressed through this manual is my lack of confidence in the maths and sciences. I am a language arts and history person. I am confident in these areas and enjoy them immensely.

As a result of my personal strengths and weaknesses, the English and history sections are much longer than the sections on math and science. (There are also many more resources available for English and history.) I could have used other people's recommendations in math and science, but have tried to stick as much as possible with what I have used personally or with what I know is popular with our customers.

In the seven years I have worked with people in the Scroll's home school department, I have felt both consolation and relief to know many people are like me. I hope others who struggle with math and science will find in my course recommendations products that will work for them. I know the least painful ways to teach these subjects!

For those math and science geniuses that are disappointed that there is no creativity and bold direction in these areas, I apologize. You should also be relieved and thankful I offered no original (and ill-informed) opinions. Your instincts are much better than mine!

SOCIAL STUDIES COURSES

Social studies refers to a wide variety of courses. History, geography, government, economics, and worldview studies all fall within this broad category. We will look at course suggestions for all of these areas.

Geography is the first area considered. Recommendations include both project and textbook suggestions.

World and church history are next, followed by American history. Both textbook and living book approaches are included. Supplementing textbook approaches with living books can add to the interest of a course. If using living books exclusively, consider using a time line or textbook to provide a framework for your course. This can be read by the student or used as a reference.

At the end of the world and American history sections are lists of nonfiction and historical fiction books worthy of your consideration. Not every book recommended is challenging. If a book is interesting and has an appealing story or presentation, the student may remember more than when using a more difficult book. Learning can take place under enjoyable conditions, too!

History is followed by government and economics courses. All suggestions are conservative promoting self-responsibility, limited government, and free market economics. Use these courses to help build your teen into a thoughtful, responsible American citizen.

Another important area is worldview studies*. Worldview studies will help your teen understand both his Christian faith and the underlying premises of philosophies opposed to Christianity. This serves a twofold purpose. First of all, it will ground your student in his faith in preparation for those who might seek to destroy it. Secondly, it will equip him to both defend and share his faith in the world's vast arena of ideas. This equipping is important even if your teen will be attending a Christian college. Many schools retain the name Christian but have left orthodox Christian belief behind.

Worldview courses can be credited as Bible, philosophy, or social study electives.

How Do We Approach the Teaching of History as Christians?

The study of history, more than science or math, is the study of opinions. We all evaluate life through a filter of basic ideas that we hold to be true. Historians, whether writing today or hundreds of years ago, have their presuppositions, too.

The accuracy of a historian's observations will be directly related to the accuracy of his presuppositions. He will interpret events in a manner supporting his viewpoints. He may fail to even mention evidence that would contradict his basic ideas.

A historian's view of God is a presupposition that will strongly affect his interpretation of history. When a historian has a high view of God's sovereignty, all of history becomes an unfolding of God's purposes in time. Earthly woes become a part of the cosmic war waged against God's purposes.

The Christian historian recognizes that this world's history is on a horizontal time line with a beginning in creation and a glorious eternal culmination. He acknowledges God's active involvement with His world, that *"the king's heart is in the hand of the Lord, like the rivers of water; He turns it wherever He wishes (Proverbs 21:1)."* The Christian historian also recognizes that he, as a mortal, is unable to delve into the depths of God's intentions, understanding the truth of Romans 11:34, *"for who has known the mind of the Lord? Or who has become His counselor?"*

In contrast, humanistic historians leave God's overarching plan out of the unfolding historical drama. History then becomes a meaningless cycle of events or a march of random occurrences driven by no power higher than man himself.

A second pertinent presupposition is the historian's view of man. The Christian historian realizes man is a fallen creature and that history is a tale of that depravity in action. Gloriously, it is also a record of God responding to that depravity with mercy, preserving a people unto Himself. That record is best discovered by reading the Christian's first historical document, the Bible. The continuation of that story is found in the centuries-long and still unfolding drama of church history.

The humanistic historian sees man as whole and valuable without God. Man is his own master capable of choosing and doing good without any aid from a god who may not exist anyway. History becomes a record of man's achievements. Although remarkable achievements do exist, one also sees cruel grasps at power with little concern for the common man. When such a historian views man sunk deep in barbarity toward his fellowman, he has no good explanation for these actions. How can such a view lead to anything but pessimism?

Read history thoughtfully and cautiously. Read to determine the historian's basic beliefs. When you have discovered them, evaluate his message and judge his accuracy in the light of that knowledge. An excellent new book, *More Than Dates & Dead People* by Stephen Mansfield (Cumberland House), teaches a Christian interpretation of history. His sense of humor and easy-to-follow writing style makes this a great choice for our history students.

WORLD GEOGRAPHY

Course: **Remedial World Geography**   Grade: **9-12**   Prerequisite: **none**

World Geography and You, Book One & Two, Steck Vaughn
▸ Teacher helps: teacher's edition with answers
▸ Description: These geography books are offered for the student who is reading significantly below grade level. They contain core content for world geography at an easier reading level.

Course: **World Geography**   Grade: **9-12**   Prerequisite: **none**

Comprehensive World Reference Guide, Instructional Fair
The World: Blank Map Forms, Evan Moor
or ***The Geography Color Book***, Kapit/Addison Wesley
a world map
The Continents, Good Year Books
GeoSafari: Geography, Educational Insights
▸ Teacher helps: none
▸ Description: Using the recommended books (and perhaps the Internet), the student will create a notebook consisting of reports and maps of countries of the world. *The Continents* is a book of world geography puzzles that can be added for variety. *GeoSafari Geography* software adds a computer drill program to the course. This is a good approach for the teen who learns best by doing or for a change of pace from textbooks.

Course: **World Geography**   Grade: **9-12**   Prerequisite: **none**

Ultimate Geography and Timeline Guide, Maggie Hogan & Cindy Wiggers, Geography Matters
▸ Teacher helps: teacher's guide only, no student book
▸ Description: This is a parent's guide for setting up an individualized geography curriculum. It is more work than other materials, but it can be used to plan your geography for all age levels. It includes geography facts, lesson and activity ideas, ideas for integrating geography into other subjects, and reproducible maps and activity sheets. Figures for a historical timeline are also included.

Course: **World Geography**   Grade: **9-12**   Prerequisite: **none**

Around the World in 180 Days, Sherri Payne, Apologia
▸ Teacher helps: teacher's guide
▸ Description: This innovative product is a multilevel listing, continent by continent, of geography and history questions for students to research. The teacher's guide contains answers and suggested resources. Student worksheets are hole-punched for creating a study notebook.

Course: **World Geography**   Grade: **7-12**   Prerequisite: **none**

Geography Lifepac Select, Alpha Omega
▸ Teacher helps: teacher's guide
▸ Description: Alpha Omega *Select* electives are lifepacs topically chosen to create a one semester course. Since the course includes both junior high and high school level lifepacs, it will be less challenging than some other choices.

World Geography (cont'd)

Course: **World Geography**	Grade: **9-12**	Prerequisite: **none**

Geography, Bob Jones University Press
Geography Student Activities Book, Bob Jones University Press
Geography Map Exercises, Bob Jones University Press
▸ Teacher helps: teacher's edition, tests and key, teacher's edition to student activities, map exercises key
▸ Description: This full color hardbound edition was revised in 1998. In addition to the text, a student activities book and map exercises are also available. Using all the supplements would make this a challenging college preparatory class.

Course: **Geography**	Grade: **6-12**	Prerequisite: **none**

Wonderful World of Geography, Runkle Publishers
Student Activity Book, Runkle Publishers
▸ Teacher helps: teacher's guide
▸ Description: This full color hardback geography text is rapidly gaining recognition in the home school community. Touted as geography's equivalent to Saxon math's incremental approach, it has received excellent reviews. An enjoyable writing style and attractive visuals are two of its noteworthy features. A separate student activity workbook is also part of the program.

WORLD HISTORY

Course: **Remedial World History**	Grade: **9-12**	Prerequisite: **none**

World History and You, **Book One & Two**, Steck Vaughn
▸ Teacher helps: teacher's edition with answers
▸ Description: These history books are offered for the student who is reading significantly below grade level. They contain core content for world history at an easier reading level.

Course: **World History**	Grade: **all grades**	Prerequisite: **none**

What in the World's Going on Here?, Diana Waring, History Alive
▸ Teacher helps: two tape sets, accompanying unit study books
▸ Description: This unit study sets the stage with informational audio tapes. Unit study books then provide a variety of follow-up activities. The course, recommended for grades four and up, surveys world history from ancient times through World War II. High schoolers will need to choose activities and books that reflect high school level work.

Course: **Ancient World History**	Grade: **9-12**	Prerequisite: **none**

Ancient History: A Literature Approach, Beautiful Feet Books
selected living books
▸ Teacher helps: teacher's guide
▸ Description: This teacher's guide presents a study of ancient history through the reading of excellent literature. Necessary literature may be purchased or oftentimes can be borrowed from the library.

| *Course:* **Medieval History** | *Grade:* **9-12** | *Prerequisite:* **none** |

Medieval, Reformation, and Renaissance History: A Literature Approach, Beautiful Feet Books
selected living books
- ▸ Teacher helps: teacher's guide, timeline
- ▸ Description: Use this guide to study medieval history through the reading of excellent classic literature. Necessary literature may be purchased or borrowed from the library.

| *Course:* **Independent Reading** (World History) | *Grade:* **9-12** | *Prerequisite:* **none** |

selected living books
- ▸ Teacher helps: none
- ▸ Description: An independent reading course can be used to study a particular historical time period. Using a historical timetable or textbook as a framework, plan an independent reading course using a variety of original documents, nonfiction, and historical fiction books. Use a time record for evaluation. A research paper would be an appropriate requirement. Check the nonfiction and historical fiction lists at the end of this section for suggestions.

| *Course:* **World History** | *Grade:* **10** | *Prerequisite:* **none** |

History and Geography Lifepacs 1001-1010, Alpha Omega
- ▸ Teacher helps: teacher's guide
- ▸ Description: The tenth grade Alpha Omega lifepacs cover world history from the ancient world to modern times. Like all of Alpha Omega's core subjects 3rd through 12th grade, this course is also available in *Switched on Schoolhouse*.

| *Course:* **World History** | *Grade:* **9-12** | *Prerequisite:* **none** |

Streams of Civilization, *Volumes One & Two*, Christian Liberty Press
- ▸ Teacher helps: teacher's guide, tests
- ▸ Description: The first volume presents world history from creation up to the Reformation. Volume II begins where Volume I left off and continues to modern times. These are inexpensive but attractive hardbound books. Teacher helps are very reasonably priced. Using one volume a year would make this course of average difficulty. Using both texts in one year would create a very rigorous college preparatory class. Adding reading selections from the world history reading lists (at the end of this section) would bring additional interest.

| *Course:* **World History** | *Grade:* **9-12** | *Prerequisite:* **none** |

World History, Bob Jones University Press
World History Student Activities Book, Bob Jones University Press
World History Map Exercises, Bob Jones University Press
- ▸ Teacher helps: teacher's edition, teacher's edition for student activity book, map packet, tests and key, *Testbuilder* software
- ▸ Description: Surveys history from creation to modern times including church history. It is a full color, hardbound book like most of BJUP texts. Using the text with tests and keys would make this of average difficulty. If adding the activity and map exercise book consider this a more rigorous college preparatory course. Adding reading selections from the world history reading lists (at the end of this section) would bring additional interest.

CHURCH HISTORY

| *Course:* **Church History** | *Grade:* **9-12** | *Prerequisite:* **none** |

Christian History Made Easy, Rose Publishing
▸ Teacher helps: leader's guide contained in book
▸ Description: This text provides a thirteen week beginner's course in church history. Supplementary activities are included. Web sites for further information are also suggested. This book along with supplementary reading, book reports, and research papers could make an interesting independent reading course in church history.

| *Course:* **Church History** | *Grade:* **9-12** | *Prerequisite:* **none** |

History of Christianity, Vision Video
▸ Teacher helps: guide, student worksheets
▸ Description: This excellent video series, in six half hour segments, presents an overview of 2000 years of church history. See Vision Video's Web site, www.visionvideo.com, for complete information.

| *Course:* **Church History** | *Grade:* **9-12** | *Prerequisite:* **none** |

Sketches from Church History, S.M. Houghton, Banner of Truth
▸ Teacher helps: none required
▸ Description: This text along with supplementary reading, book reports, and research papers could make an excellent independent reading course in church history.

| *Course:* **Church History** | *Grade:* **9-12** | *Prerequisite:* **none** |

The Church in History, B. K. Kuiper, Eerdmans
▸ Teacher helps: end of chapter questions but no answer key
The Story of Liberty, Charles Coffman, Maranatha
▸ Teacher helps: study guide available
▸ Description: A survey of the Christian church through the ages. *The Story Of Liberty's* story approach is interesting to read alongside the main text.

WORLD HISTORY: NON-FICTION

With so much of early history a probable combination of fact and myth, most of the suggested reading for Greece and Rome is in historical fiction.

Timetables of History, Simon & Schuster
▸ Description: A timetable with yearly listings on what was happening in history, literature, religion, music, science, etc. A timetable can serve as a framework for a history course using living books.

Timelines of World History, EDC Publishing, Usborne Books
▸ Description: This colorful illustrated timeline will not have the thoroughness of the timeline above; this may make it easier to concentrate on key events if you are using it as a framework for an independent reading course.

Kingfisher History Encyclopedia, Kingfisher Publishing
▸ Description: This huge book takes you on an interesting walk through history. The book is heavily illustrated and has an attractive presentation. This could serve as a framework for a history course using living books.

The World's Great Speeches, Copeland, Lamm, & McKenna; Dover
▸ Description: This book contains 292 speeches representing nearly every historical era and nation. A helpful reference of original documents.

The Christian Almanac, George Grant, Cumberland House
▸ Description: A two page spread for each day of the year includes an essay about a significant occurrence on that day in history, a list of other important events, and an inspiring quotation, all from a Christian perspective.

The Story of Christianity, Matthew A. Price and Michael Collins, Tyndale House
▸ Description: This colorful oversized book offers both an interesting and readable text.

The 100 Most Important Events in Christian History, A. Kenneth Curtis, J. Stephen Lang, and Randy Peterson; Revell
▸ Description: An overview of important events in church history. This would be an excellent supplement to a world history course.

Turning Points, Mark A. Knoll, Baker
▸ Description: A presentation of twelve decisive moments in church history.

Trial and Triumph, Richard Hannula, Canon Press
▸ Description: In forty-six brief biographies Hannula introduces the reader to the trials and triumphs of various well-known and lesser-known Christians of the past. Written in an easy-to-read style the whole family can enjoy.

Then and Now Bible Maps, Rose Publishing
▸ Description: Seven Bible maps have transparent overlays showing the Holy Lands today. A helpful study aid.

Genesis, Ruth Beechick, available from Mott Media
▸ Description: Ruth Beechick has written a fascinating book suggesting some very plausible ideas pertaining to the book of Genesis.

Trial and Testimony of the Early Church, Vision Video
▸ Description: This set of two videos, containing six half hour segments, presents the history of the early church. This award-winning docudrama also includes a teacher's guide, worksheets and book.

WORLD HISTORY: NON-FICTION (CONT'D)

The History of the Church, Eusebius
▸ Description: Eusebius (AD 263-339) is often called "the father of ecclesiastical history." This is the only surviving account of the early Christian church.

Ecclesiastical History of the English People, Bede
▸ Description: The venerable Bede (673-733), a Benedictine monk, relates the spread of the Christian church from Roman times until his day.

What Life Was Like..., Time-Life Books
▸ Description: This beautiful series of full color books has interesting illustrations, photographs, and text. Each book covers a different time period in world history. We have been pleased with the volume we purchased, *What Life was Like in the Age of Chivalry*. However, these fairly expensive books are not as widely available as when we purchased ours. Used bookstores might be a good source, or you might borrow them on interlibrary loan.

Famous Men of Greece (Rome, Middle Ages, Renaissance and Reformation), Greenleaf Press
▸ Description: Although targeted for a younger audience, this biographical approach to history would make a good supplement to an independent reading course.

Living History: Pyramids of Ancient Egypt, etc., Gulliver Books, Harcourt Brace Jovanovich
▸ Description: The *Living History* series are photographed reenactments of life during various time periods. These are books for the whole family with wonderful full color photographs and limited text. Not at all difficult, they will be an interesting quick read for your teen. Unfortunately, many of these books are out of print. I have been successful in finding some at used book stores. Interlibrary loan may also help you find these enjoyable family books. Look for the following titles: *Pyramids of Ancient Egypt, Ancient Greece, Classical Rome, The Vikings, The Voyages of Christopher Columbus, Fourteenth Century Towns, Knights In Armor, Italian Renaissance, First World War*, and *Industrial Revolution*.

Augustus Caesar's World, Genevieve Foster, Beautiful Feet Books
▸ Description: Learn all about Augustus Caesar and the world he lived in as you read this book. As Jesus Christ was born during the reign of Augustus Caesar, you will also be learning about the world at the time of Christ. This is an easy enjoyable read.

The Confessions of St. Augustine, Augustine
▸ Description: Follow Augustine through his life and his embracing of various philosophies of the day until his ultimate conversion to Christianity.

Let Me Die in Ireland, David Bercot, Scroll Publishing
▸ Description: A biography of St. Patrick, the early Christian missionary to Ireland. Bercot's sources included the personal letters of St. Patrick.

Reformation Overview, Vision Video
▸ Description: This set of two videos, containing six half hour segments, presents the main figures of the Reformation: Wycliffe, Hus, Luther, Zwingli, Calvin, the Anabaptists, and Tyndale. A teacher's guide and worksheets are included.

Here I Stand: A Life of Martin Luther, Robert Bainton
▸ Description: Martin Luther was one of the most important figures of the Reformation. Read of Martin Luther's life from prospective law student to monk, and then as the figure who so drastically influenced the Church at great risk to himself.

Life of John Calvin, Theodore Beza, Back Home Industries
▸ Description: John Calvin was one of the most important figures of the Reformation. He was a reticent man whose desire was to live a quiet life of scholarship. Yet God used him in a way that has borne great influence for centuries. Read history written by Calvin's close friend.

Never Give In, Stephen Mansfield, Cumberland House
▸ Description: A presentation of Churchill's life and thoughts from the *Leaders in Action* series.

Anne Frank: The Diary of a Young Girl, Anne Frank
▸ Description: Almost everyone is familiar with this poignant diary kept by a young German girl during her family's days of hiding from the Nazis during World War II.

The Hiding Place, Corrie Ten Boom
▸ Description: The moving account of Corrie Ten Boom, her sister Betsy, and their family as they participate in the Dutch resistance during World War II at the cost of their freedom. It is an inspiring account of God's providential care of His children during the worst of circumstances. Progeny Press and Alpha Omega *Lifepac 707* study this excellent autobiographical account.

Bonhoeffer: The Cost of Freedom, Focus on the Family
▸ Description: This is an audio drama of the life of Dietrich Bonhoeffer. Bonhoeffer, a German minister, was accused of treason and executed by the Nazis shortly before the end of World War II. This is another fine recording from the Focus on the Family Radio Theater.

Bonhoeffer: Agent of Grace, Gateway Films, Vision Video
▸ Description: *Bonhoeffer: Agent of Grace* is a moving film about the life of the German minister Dietrich Bonhoeffer. Safely out of Germany, he feels compelled to return to his fellow believers. After great personal struggle, he becomes involved in the resistance movement which ultimately costs him his life. (Note: the execution scene contains brief nudity viewed from the back.) Nonrated.

Not a Tame Lion, Terry W. Glaspey, Cumberland House
▸ Description: An examination of the life and unique thoughts of C.S. Lewis. This is part of the excellent *Leaders in Action* series.

WORLD HISTORY: FICTION

Books are arranged to flow chronologically through historical time periods. Most books should be easily attainable at libraries, interlibrary loan, or special ordered from bookstores. We have used the majority of these books in our home school.

Adam and His Kin, Ruth Beechick, available from Mott Media
▸ Description: A fictional but well-researched and believable presentation of Genesis.

The Golden Goblet, Eloise McGraw
▸ Description: Although a very easy read for high school, it is still an exciting and well-written book on ancient Egypt. This and *Mara* (mentioned below) are my personal favorites on Egypt.

Mara, Daughter of the Nile, Eloise McGraw
▸ Description: If you read one historical fiction book on ancient Egypt, this should be it.

Black Ships before Troy, Rosemary Sutcliff
▸ Description: A beautifully illustrated hardcover retelling of Homer's *The Iliad*. A companion volume, *The Wanderings of Odysseus*, retells *The Odyssey*.

The Iliad, Homer
▸ Description: *The Iliad* is the ancient tale of the conquering of Troy. It probably represents a combination of actual history and myth.

The Odyssey, Homer
▸ Description: *The Odyssey* describes the adventures of Odysseus on his way back from the Trojan War. It probably represents a combination of actual history and myth.

The Aeneid, Virgil
▸ Description: *The Aeneid* is the ancient poetic history of Rome.

The Eagle of the Ninth, Rosemary Sutcliff
▸ Description: In A.D. 119 the Ninth Roman Legion marched north into the wilds of Britain and never returned. This is the exciting tale of the search for clues to their fate and the effort to find their eagle standard. The historical disappearance of the Ninth Legion without a trace and the finding of the lost standard in an archaeological dig are the factual basis for this exciting story.

The Silver Branch, Rosemary Sutcliff
▸ Description: A story of intrigue as a young army surgeon and his soldier cousin discover a plot against the British emperor. Another excellent story of Roman Britain.

The Lantern Bearers, Rosemary Sutcliff
▸ Description: When Rome can no longer maintain its position against the barbaric invaders of Britain, the defenders abandon their posts and return to Rome. Aquila, a young legionnaire stays behind to fight the invaders and try to save the land. If you enjoy Rosemary Sutcliff as much as we have, you will want to read two more of her books on Roman Britain, *The Outcast* and *The Shining Company*.

The Dragonslayer, Rosemary Sutcliff
▸ Description: A retelling of the ancient European tale Beowulf.

The Bronze Bow, Elizabeth Speare
▸ Description: Young Jewish Daniel belongs to a group rebelling against Roman rule in Israel. He is confronted with Jesus' followers and stories of the Christ. Daniel must decide how to handle the hatred so imbedded in his heart. A Newbery Award book, it portrays Daniel's agony as he rethinks his hatred. Progeny Press has a guide for this book.

A Journey of Souls, C.D. Baker, Preston Speed
▶ Description: The story of three children who join the ill-fated children's crusade (1212) to free Jerusalem from the Turks.

The Scottish Chiefs, Jane Porter
▶ Description: A tale of the Scottish fight for independence from England. The book's focus is on William Wallace.

Adam of the Road, Elizabeth Gray
▶ Description: A young boy in Medieval England, Adam takes to the road searching for his minstrel father. His travels give a varied and accurate picture of life at that time. An easy and enjoyable Newbery Award book.

Men of Iron, Howard Pyle
▶ Description: Any boy interested in knights will enjoy this book. Myles trains to be a knight, vindicates his father from unjust suspicions, wins a bride, and battles both his own temperament and enemies. This book is considered one of the outstanding books on medieval England.

Otto of the Silver Hand, Howard Pyle
▶ Description: A tale of the son of a valiant robber baron in Medieval Germany. Gentle Otto, raised in a monastery, returns home to feuds between his house and a rival baron. If you enjoy this Howard Pyle book (we did!), you have many more medieval tales to choose from. Other titles by Howard Pyle include *The Story of King Arthur and His Knights* and *Robin Hood*.

The Black Arrow, Robert Louis Stevenson
▶ Description: *The Black Arrow* is set in England during the War of the Roses with the suffering that war brings to all sides clearly seen in the story.

Outlaws of Sherwood, Robin McKinley
▶ Description: A modern retelling of Robin Hood and his merry men. An enjoyable read.

Ivanhoe, Sir Walter Scott
▶ Description: A classic tale of medieval adventure well-seasoned with actual historical figures. *Rob Roy* and *The Talisman* have also been read at our home. Sir Walter Scott is appreciated by one of our teens.

A Parcel of Patterns, Jill Paten Walsh
▶ Description: Mall Percival is a teen, soon to be adult, telling the story of the dreadful years when her village was struck by the plague. A very powerful and well-written story, based on the true story of how Eyam, England, was devastated by the plague in 1665. I highly recommend it.

The Trumpeter of Krakow, Eric Kelly
▶ Description: Another Medieval story, but this one is set in Poland. The hero of an exciting adventure story, young Joseph must protect the Great Tarnov crystal against the plundering Tartars.

The Second Mrs. Giaconda, E.L. Konigsberg
▶ Description: A story of Renaissance Italy, Leonardo de Vinci, and his rapscallion young apprentice. The story closes with the painting of the Mona Lisa.

I, Juan de Pareja, Elizabeth Trevino
▶ Description: Another story of the Renaissance, Juan is the slave of the Spanish court painter, Diego Velasquez. Daily he watches the master paint, learning as he watches. Juan secretly begins to paint, a forbidden activity for a slave. This is a Newbery Award book.

The Scarlet Pimpernel, Baroness Orczy
▶ Description: Set during the French Revolution, the Scarlet Pimpernel, an elusive and daring Englishman, snatches French nobility away from the danger of the guillotine. Chauvelin has sworn to stop him.

WORLD HISTORY: FICTION (CONT'D)

A Tale of Two Cities, Charles Dickens
‣ Description: This is a poignant story about the French Revolution. The ending is particularly memorable. Progeny Press has a guide for this book.

All Quiet on the Western Front, Eric Remarque
‣ Description: This is a popular high school choice for World War I historical fiction.

The Endless Steppe, Esther Hautzig
‣ Description: In this World War II story Esther, her mother, and grandmother struggle for survival as they are transported from Poland to Siberia.

Escape from Warsaw, Ian Serraillier
‣ Description: A World War II story about four children escaping from the Jewish ghetto in Warsaw, Poland.

The Zion Covenant Series, Bodie Thoene
‣ Description: This adult Christian series by Bodie Thoene is set in Europe before and during World War II.

Life Is Beautiful, Miramax Home Entertainment
‣ Description: This award-winning Italian-made movie is a poignant story of one young couple's happiness threatened by World War II. The ensuing story finds them living separated lives in a concentration camp. The father creates heartwarming (and heart-wrenching) little games to hide the truth of their desperate existence from his little son. I recommend watching the Italian version with the English captions. Losing the beauty of the Italian language in order to get dubbed English is too great a sacrifice. Rated PG-13.

G.A. Henty Books

George Alfred Henty (1832-1902) was a prolific writer of historical adventures which were well-respected for their historical accuracy. Critics of the day sometimes criticized his characters as being "too Christian," thus making them a great fit for the home school market! PrestonSpeed has reprinted the Henty titles below with more planned. Check their Web site, prestonspeed.com, for descriptions of each book and information on the various editions available. The chronological chart below will help you locate a Henty book for your studies. At least one historical figure appears in most of the books.

Title	Date	Description	Famous Character
The Cat of Bubastes	1250 BC	Egypt during the reign of Thutmose III	Moses
The Young Carthaginian	220 BC	2nd Punic War	Hannibal
For the Temple	70 BC	Fall of Jerusalem	Josephus
Beric the Briton	61 BC	Roman invasion of Britain	
The Dragon and the Raven	870 AD	Viking invasions of England	King Alfred
Wulf the Saxon	1066	Norman Conquest	William the Conqueror
Winning His Spurs	1190	Third Crusade	Richard the Lionhearted
In Freedom's Cause	1314	Scottish Rebellion	Robert the Bruce William Wallace
St. George for England	1340	Hundred Years' War	Edward, the Black Prince of Wales
The Lion of St. Mark	1380	Venice, Italy at her height	
A March on London	1381	Wat Tyler's Insurrection	Wat Tyler
The Knight of the White Cross	1480	First Siege of Rhodes	Knights of St. John Order
By Pike and Dyke	1579	The Dutch fight for freedom	William the Silent
St. Bartholomew's Eve	1580	Huguenot Wars	Coligny, Queen Elizabeth, etc.
Under Drake's Flag	1580	the Spanish Main	Sir Francis Drake
By England's Aid	1588	Dutch fight for freedom cont.	Sir Francis Vere
By Right of Conquest	1595	Spanish conquest of Mexico	Cortez
The Lion of the North	1630	30 Years' War	King Gustavus Adolphus of Sweden
Won by the Sword	1640	30 Years' War	Richelieu
Bonnie Prince Charlie	1745	Battle of Culloden	Charles Edward Stuart
With Wolfe in Canada	1759	French and Indian War	George Washington
In the Reign of Terror	1793	French Revolution	
The Tiger of Mysore	1795	Mysore War in India	
Under Wellington's Command	1810	Peninsular War	Wellington
With Lee in Virginia	1860's	American Civil War	Robert E. Lee
The Dash for Khartoum	1885	Siege of Khartoum	
Facing Death	Victorian era	Welsh coal mines	

AMERICAN HISTORY

Course: **Remedial American History**   *Grade:* **9-12**   *Prerequisite:* **none**

America's History: Land of Liberty, Book One & Two, Steck Vaughn
▸ Teacher helps: teacher's edition with answers
▸ Description: These history books are offered for the student reading significantly below grade level. They contain core content for American history at an easier reading level.

Course: **American History**   *Grade:* **9-12**   *Prerequisite:* **none**

A History of Us, Volumes 1-10, Joy Hakim, Oxford University Press
▸ Teacher helps: none required
▸ Description: If you have a student who dislikes history, these books may change his mind. These highly interesting history "storybooks" do at times express some of the author's non-conservative views (especially volumes one and ten) so be prepared for discussion. Written on a junior high level, these books may work well as a framework, adding more living books to make the course more challenging. A research paper in an area where the student's opinion differs from the author's wouldn't be a bad idea either.

Course: **American History**   *Grade:* **9-12**   *Prerequisite:* **none**

The Landmark History of the American People, Daniel Boorstin, Sonlight Curriculum
▸ Teacher helps: none
▸ Description: This interesting history focuses on how people both great and small came together to form America. Boorstin's easy-to-read approach directs the reader to the big picture rather than losing him in the details. This family favorite would make an excellent foundation for an independent reading course.

Course: **American History**   *Grade:* **9-12**   *Prerequisite:* **none**

Literature Approach to U.S. and World History, Beautiful Feet Books
▸ Teacher helps: teacher's guide
▸ Description: A literature approach to the study of history from the 1860's to 1970's (Civil War to the Vietnam War). The teacher's guide directs you through the study with vocabulary, comprehension questions, etc. Literature is purchased separately.

Course: **Independent Reading** (American Hist.)   *Grade:* **9-12**   *Prerequisite:* **none**

selected living books
▸ Teacher helps: none
▸ Description: An independent reading course can be used to study a particular historical time period. Using a historical timetable or textbook as a framework, plan an independent reading course using a variety of original documents, nonfiction, and historical fiction books. Use a time record for evaluation. A research paper would be an appropriate requirement. Check the following nonfiction and historical fiction listings for suggestions.

Course: **American History**   *Grade:* **9-12**   *Prerequisite:* **none**

A New World in View, Reformation to Colonization, Gary DeMar, American Vision
▸ Teacher helps: packet includes teacher's guide, tests, and key
▸ Description: These first two books in the *To Pledge Allegiance* series (more books are planned) begin on an Old World stage and proceed through colonization. These excellent junior high books could serve as a framework for an independent reading course in American history

Course: **American History**   *Grade:* **11**   *Prerequisite:* **none**

History and Geography Lifepacs 1101-1110, Alpha Omega
▸ Teacher helps: teacher's guide
▸ Description: The eleventh grade Alpha Omega lifepacs cover American history. Like all of Alpha Omega's core subjects 3rd through 12th grade, this course is also available in *Switched on Schoolhouse*.

Course: **American History**   *Grade:* **9-12**   *Prerequisite:* **none**

United States History, Bob Jones University Press
United States History Student Activities Book, Bob Jones University Press
United States Map Exercises, Bob Jones University Press
▸ Teacher helps: teacher's edition, teacher's edition for activity book, map packet, tests, *Testbuilder* software
▸ Description: A survey of American history from the discoverers to the present which integrates some American church history. An attractive full color hardbound book. Using the text with tests makes it of average difficulty. Using the activity book and map packet makes this a solid college preparatory course. Adding reading selections from our American history reading lists would add both interest and challenge. These selections are listed at the end of this section.

Course: **American History**   *Grade:* **9-12**   *Prerequisite:* **none**

A Basic History of the United States, **six volume set**, American Textbook Committee
▸ Teacher helps: teacher's guide with questions, well-organized but no answer key
▸ Description: Written by Clarence Carson, this course will provide a conservative approach to the study of American history. We have found Clarence Carson to be very readable. The teacher's guide was very helpful in identifying main ideas, people, etc., for highlighting and study. Adding a research paper or reading selections from the American history reading lists would make this course even more challenging. These selections are listed at the end of this section.

AMERICAN HISTORY: NON-FICTION

America's God and Country, Wm. Federer
 ▶ Description: An encyclopedia of quotations which highlights the noble heritage of America.

The Patriot's Handbook, George Grant, Cumberland House
 ▶ Description: A handbook full of patriotic poems and prose.

The Pocket Patriot, George Grant, Cumberland House
 ▶ Description: A little "primer" for American citizens. Contents include historical documents, speeches, and short sketches on each president.

Our Country's Founders, William Bennett
 ▶ Description: The virtues of our founding fathers are presented through poems, letters, speeches, and articles. The adult version of this book, *Our Sacred Honor*, is also available.

To the Best of My Ability, James M. McPherson, Dorling Kindersley
 ▶ Description: In this excellent reference book, six pages of full color photographs and biographical information are included for each president. A very readable and fascinating book.

Critical Thinking in United States History, Critical Thinking Press
 ▶ Description: If you like lively discussions, this series will serve as an excellent catalyst. Students are presented with opposing interpretations of controversial historical events often using excerpts from original documents. The challenge is to analyze the data and try to arrive at accurate conclusions. Students will soon see that the "facts" are not as objective as they seem.

America's Christian History: The Untold Story, Gary DeMar, American Vision
 ▶ Description: This is a carefully researched book presenting the Christian roots of our nation. An audio presentation is also available.

The Story of Liberty, Charles Coffin, Maranatha or Mantle Ministries
 ▶ Description: This highly readable story tells the progress of liberty beginning with the signing of the Magna Carta up to the discovery of America. This is a worthwhile companion for any study in church or world history. Study guide available.

Sweet Land of Liberty (Mantle uses the original title, **Old Times in the Colonies**.), Charles Coffin, Maranatha or Mantle Ministries
 ▶ Description: This is a sequel to *The Story of Liberty* ending after the French and Indian War. Charles Coffin's storytelling is very readable.

America: The First 350 Years, J. Steven Wilkins, Covenant Publications
 ▶ Description: Listening to these tapes will blow the cobwebs out of your mind as you develop a new perspective on American history. Full of anecdotal stories and facts you were probably never taught in school, these tapes are both Christian and carefully researched. Each of the 16 tapes is 45 minutes long. A notebook containing course notes is also included. Our family has greatly enjoyed these tapes.

World of Columbus and Sons, Genevieve Foster, Beautiful Feet Books
 ▶ Description: Genevieve Foster's books study individuals in a way uniquely her own. As you learn of Columbus you will also learn what was happening in the world in which he lived.

Empires Lost and Won: The Spanish Heritage in the Southwest, Albert Marrin, Atheneum
 ▶ Description: Albert Marrin is a remarkable storyteller, making history come alive for his readers. We are using this book as part of our study of Texas.

The World of Captain John Smith, Genevieve Foster, Beautiful Feet Books
  ▸ Description: Learn about Captain John Smith and the world in which he lived.

Of Plymouth Plantation, William Bradford, Mantle Ministries
  ▸ Description: A very readable history of Plymouth written by the godly man who was governor for almost forty years. You can't study colonial America thoroughly without at least reading excerpts from this.

Sea King: Sir Francis Drake and His Time, Albert Marrin
  ▸ Description: Albert Marrin is a remarkable storyteller, making history come alive for his readers. Marrin has written over 20 books for young readers; unfortunately, not all of them are now in print. If you like to wander used bookstores, put him on your list of authors to look for.

George Washington's World, Genevieve Foster, Beautiful Feet Books
  ▸ Description: Read about George Washington and find out what was happening elsewhere in the world during his lifetime.

The Autobiography of Benjamin Franklin, Benjamin Franklin
  ▸ Description: The autobiography of one of the most influential men in colonial America.

Poor Richard, James Daugherty, Beautiful Feet Books
  ▸ Description: An older popular biography of Benjamin Franklin republished in recent years.

Give Me Liberty, David Vaughan, Cumberland House
  ▸ Description: Learn all about Patrick Henry, his life, and his thoughts in this biography from the *Leaders in Action* series.

The Boys of '76, Mantle Ministries
  ▸ Description: A third title by Charles Coffin, this one on the Revolutionary War. If you enjoy Coffin's style, you will be pleased that Mantle Ministries has plans to republish four more American history titles by Coffin.

A Young Patriot, Jim Murphy, Clarion
  ▸ Description: The Revolutionary War as seen through the eyes of a fifteen year old American soldier.

Best Little Stories from the American Revolution, C. Brian Kelly, Cumberland House
  ▸ Description: If you like these little historical vignettes, C. Brian Kelly has three other "best little" books on the Civil War, the White House, and World War II.

The Federalist Papers, Hamilton, Madison, Jay
  ▸ Description: During the formation period of the United States, these papers were written by ardent defenders of a strong central government.

The Anti-federalist Papers, Ralph Ketcham
  ▸ Description: The less well-known *Anti-federalist Papers* give the views of those opposing a strong centralized government for the new nation.

Jonathan Edwards: A New Biography, Ian Murray
  ▸ Description: A well-known biography of Jonathan Edwards written for adults but very readable.

Jonathan and Sarah: An Uncommon Union, Edna Gerstner, Soli Deo Gloria
  ▸ Description: A look at the private life of Jonathan Edwards carefully researched from Edwards family diaries and journals.

A Burning and Shining Light, Denise C. Stubbs, Soli Deo Gloria
  ▸ Description: This is the biography of David Brainerd, close friend to Jonathan Edwards and missionary to the Indians. For the more ambitious reader, see Jonathan Edward's biography, *The Life and Diary of David Brainerd*.

AMERICAN HISTORY: NON-FICTION (CONT'D)

The Journals of Lewis and Clark, edited by Frank Bergon, Penguin
▶ Description: The journals of Meriwether Lewis and William Clarks' eight thousand mile journey (1804-1806) from the Missouri River to the Pacific Ocean.

Of Courage Undaunted, James Daugherty, Beautiful Feet Books
▶ Description: An older, popular narrative of the Lewis and Clark expedition, republished in recent years.

Democracy in America, Alexis de Tocqueville
▶ Description: America as seen through the eyes of a French statesman visiting our country in the 1830's. It is a penetrating view of American society and its character. It may be more practical to read excerpts rather than attempt the whole book.

Cowboys, Indians, and Gunfighter: The Story of the Cattle Kingdom, Albert Marrin
▶ Description: Albert Marrin is a remarkable storyteller, making history come alive for his readers. Marrin has written over 20 books for young readers; unfortunately, not all of them are now in print. If you like to wander used bookstores, put him on your list of authors to look for.

The Raven, Marquis James
▶ Description: This excellent biography of Sam Houston gives valuable insight into the settling of the American West.

Abraham Lincoln's World, Genevieve Foster, Beautiful Feet Books
▶ Description: Genevieve Foster's books study individuals in a way uniquely her own. As you learn of Lincoln, you will also learn what was happening in the world in which he lived.

Abraham Lincoln: A Photobiography, Russell Freedman
▶ Description: Freedman's excellent book won the Newbery Award.

Daily Life on a Southern Plantation, Paul Erickson
▶ Description: Text, photographs, maps, etc., all help you taste life on a Louisiana plantation.

To Be a Slave, Julius Lester
▶ Description: Slavery as seen through the eyes of former slaves.

Up from Slavery, Booker T. Washington
▶ Description: The autobiography of Booker T. Washington, former slave, famous black educator, and Christian. It was a privilege meeting this truly great man in the pages of his book.

Then Darkness Fled, Stephen Mansfield, Cumberland House
▶ Description: A biography of Booker T. Washington, the former slave, famous black educator, and Christian. Another excellent choice in the *Leaders in Action* series.

The Boy's War, Jim Murphy, Clarion Books
▶ Description: The Civil War seen through the eyes of the young men who fought.

The Long Road to Gettysburg, Jim Murphy, Clarion Books
▶ Description: First hand accounts of the Battle of Gettysburg seen through the eyes of the war's young soldiers. Jim Murphy's books have won a variety of prestigious awards.

The Civil War, Public Broadcasting System
▶ Description: This excellent nine volume video series produced by Ken Burns in 1991 can sometimes be rented at video stores, or check your library's video collection.

A Call to Duty, J. Steven Wilkins, Cumberland House
▸ Description: This volume from the *Leaders in Action* series is a combination biography and study of Robert E. Lee's character.

Life of JEB Stuart, Mary L. Williamson, Christian Liberty Press
▸ Description: This attractive new edition tells the story of General JEB Stuart who was in charge of the cavalry of the Confederate army.

Life of Stonewall Jackson, Mary L. Williamson, Christian Liberty Press
▸ Description: This attractive new edition from Christian Liberty Press tells the story of the heroic Stonewall Jackson. An asset to Lee's Confederate army, Stonewall Jackson was also a fine Christian man.

The Great Fire, Jim Murphy, Scholastic
▸ Description: A photobiography of the great Chicago fire of 1871. This was a Newbery Honor book.

Blizzard!, Jim Murphy, Scholastic
▸ Description: Another Jim Murphy book, this one about a blizzard that paralyzed New York City on March 12, 1888.

Carry a Big Stick, George Grant, Cumberland House
▸ Description: This is a biography of Theodore Roosevelt from the excellent *Leaders in Action* series.

Farewell to Manzanar, Jeanne Wakatsuki Houston
▸ Description: The story of a Japanese-American girl and her family's life in an internment camp in California during World War II.

AMERICAN HISTORY: FICTION

> *This section contains historical fiction set in America. The table flows chronologically through historical time periods. Most books should be easily attainable at libraries, interlibrary loan, or special ordered from bookstores. We have used the majority of these books in our home school.*

The Witch of Blackbird Pond, Elizabeth George Speare
▸ Description: Set in Puritan New England during the witch scare, Kit comes to live with her Puritan cousins. Through her strong-willed behavior a woman is imprisoned for witchcraft. This Newbery Award book has a wonderful depth to its characterizations and is not just Puritan bashing (a popular American pastime). Progeny Press has a guide for this book.

The Scarlet Letter, Nathanial Hawthorne
▸ Description: The Scarlet Letter is the story of Hester Prynne, condemned by her Puritan community for bearing her daughter, Pearl, out of wedlock. The story proceeds through Hester's life as an outcast until the public confession of a dying Roger Dimmesdale. Hawthorne's short novel is often studied at the high school level. Progeny Press publishes a guide for this novel.

Johnny Tremain, Esther Forbes
▸ Description: The abiding tale of Johnny Tremain, an apprentice silversmith, who lives in Boston during the days preceding the revolution. You will meet many of the revolutionary heroes on the pages of this book. I have read this book three times, twice out loud. A Progeny Press guide is available for this book.

Traitor: The Case of Benedict Arnold, Jean Fritz
▸ Description: Jean Fritz books are always a treat because of their unique approach to history. This book for older students is the story of American patriot turned traitor, Benedict Arnold.

Streams to the River, River to the Sea, Scott O'Dell
▸ Description: This is the story of Sacajawea, the young Indian girl who guided Lewis and Clark on their western exploration of America.

The Oregon Trail, Francis Parkman
▸ Description: We need at least one western adventure book!

Slave Dancer, Paula Fox
▸ Description: A young boy is kidnapped and taken to sea to be a slave dancer. Read the book to find out what a slave dancer is. It is a cruel picture that you will likely never forget.

Uncle Tom's Cabin, Harriet Beecher Stowe
▸ Description: Abraham Lincoln upon receiving Harriet Beecher Stowe at the White House called her "the little woman who wrote the book that made this great war." Mrs. Stowe's description of the plight of the black slave inflamed northern sentiments. This book is a testimony to the power of the written word.

The Killer Angels, Michael Shaara
▸ Description: *The Killer Angels*, a story of the battle of Gettysburg, is considered one of the best Civil War novels ever written. This book has motivated many people to delve deeper into this very critical time period in our country's history. (The movie *Gettysburg* was based upon this book. It's excellent!)

Stonewall, John J. Dwyer
▸ Description: *Stonewall* is a novel released on the Christian market about Stonewall Jackson, the great southern general during the Civil War.

The Red Badge of Courage, Stephen Crane
▸ Description: The Civil War seen through the eyes of a young man enamored with the glories of war. We learn about war with him on the battlefield. Progeny Press has a guide for this book.

Across Five Aprils, Irene Hunt
▸ Description: Set in rural southern Illinois, the book's family is divided by the Civil War. Irene Hunt is an excellent writer.

Rifles for Watie, Harold Keith
▸ Description: An excellent book about young Jefferson Davis Bussey who joins the northern army, later becoming a spy in the southern army. Your sympathy grows for both sides of the conflict as you read through his experiences. This Civil War book, a Newbery Award winner, is mandatory reading in our home.

My Antonia, Willa Cather
▸ Description: Life on the Nebraska prairie as seen through the life of imigrant and pioneer Antonia.

A Lantern in Her Hand and ***A White Bird Flying***, Bess Streeter Aldrich
▸ Description: Bess Streeter Aldrich shows life on the prairie as it changes during the course of one woman's lifetime. Girls especially should enjoy these books.

No Promises in the Wind, Irene Hunt
▸ Description: A young boy with his friend set out on their own to ease the financial strain at home during the Depression. Irene Hunt writes an excellent story even when its honest portrayal of family struggle and sudden death is not always comfortable.

Roll of Thunder, Hear my Cry, Mildred Taylor
▸ Description: This Newbery Award book tells the story of Cassie, a young black girl growing up on a farm during the Depression. Her family struggles valiantly to maintain their integrity and independence while facing the prejudices of the day. A Progeny Press guide is available for this book.

To Kill a Mockingbird, Harper Lee
▸ Description: The absorbing story of a small southern town, the unjust imprisonment of a black man, and the white lawyer who defends him — all seen through the eyes of the lawyer's little girl. Progeny Press has a guide for this book. When you are all done, rent the old movie starring Gregory Peck. It's good, too! (Parental note: the man is accused of raping a white woman.)

AMERICAN GOVERNMENT

Course: Remedial American Government   Grade: **9-12**   Prerequisite: **American History**

American Government: Freedom, Rights, Responsibilities, Steck Vaughn
▸ Teacher helps: teacher's edition with answers
▸ Description: This government book is offered for the student who is reading significantly below grade level. It contains core content for American government at an easier reading level.

Course: Government/Economics   Grade: **9-12**   Prerequisite: **none**

The *Uncle Eric* **books**, Bluestocking Press
▸ Teacher helps: teacher's guide to *Penny Candy* only
▸ Description: Uncle Eric writes his nephew letters explaining all kinds of economic and political ideas from his very conservative viewpoint. The books in order are: *Uncle Eric Talks about Personal, Career, and Financial Security; Whatever Happened to Penny Candy?; Whatever Happened to Justice?; Are You Liberal? Conservative? Confused?; Ancient Rome: How It Affects You Today; Evaluating Books — What Would Thomas Jefferson Think About This?; Clipper Ship Strategy; Money Mystery*; and *The Thousand Year War*. These books have generated a great deal of discussion in our home.

Course: Government   Grade: **9-12**   Prerequisite: **U.S. & World Hist.**

Land of Fair Play, Christian Liberty Press
▸ Teacher helps: teacher's guide, tests & key
Our Living Constitution, Good Apple
▸ Teacher helps: answers in back of book
or *The Story of the Constitution*, Christian Liberty Press
▸ Teacher helps: teacher's manual, tests
▸ Description: *Land of Fair Play* and *Our Living Constitution* are junior high materials but are good for giving a basic understanding of our government and constitution. However, something will need to be added to make this a legitimate high school course. *The Story of the Constitution* workbook, an excellent new revision from CLP, could replace *Our Living Constitution* to create a more challenging course. Perhaps adding additional living books on governmental issues, or writing a research paper will meet the need. Bluestocking Press' *Uncle Eric* books on governmental and economic topics might be a good choice.

Course: Government   Grade: **7-12**   Prerequisite: **U.S. & World Hist.**

Civics Lifepac Select, Alpha Omega
▸ Teacher helps: teacher's guide
▸ Description: Alpha Omega *Select* electives are lifepacs topically chosen to create a one semester course. Since the courses include both junior high and high school level lifepacs, this course will be less challenging than some other choices.

Course: Government/Economics   Grade: **12**   Prerequisite: **none**

History and Geography Lifepacs 1201-1210, Alpha Omega
▸ Teacher helps: teacher's guide
▸ Description: The twelfth grade Alpha Omega lifepacs cover government and economics. Like all of Alpha Omega's core 3rd through 12th grade subjects, this course is also available in *Switched on Schoolhouse*.

| *Course:* **Government** | *Grade:* **11-12** | *Prerequisite:* **U.S. & World Hist.** |

Government, Bob Jones University Press
▸ Teacher helps: teacher's edition, tests and key, *Testbuilder* software
▸ Description: This full color hardbound book from Bob Jones University Press can be taught as a one or two semester course.

| *Course:* **U. S. Government** | *Grade:* **9-12** | *Prerequisite:* **U.S. & World Hist.** |

God and Government, Volumes 1-3, Gary Demar, American Vision
▸ Teacher helps: Volume 1 and 2 tests available from Christian Liberty Press
▸ Description: This is a very readable three volume set which builds a Christian philosophy of government in general, American government in particular. Chapters end with questions, a summarization, and answers to the questions. This series is for the student who wants to delve deeply into a Christian philosophy of government.

| *Course:* **Government** | *Grade:* **12** | *Prerequisite:* **American History** |

Basic American Government, Clarence Carson, American Textbook Committee
▸ Teacher helps: none
▸ Description: A conservative presentation of American government. The lack of teacher evaluation tools makes this course most suited for the motivated independent reader.

| *Course:* **Constitutional Law** | *Grade:* **11-12** | *Prerequisite:* **American History** |

Constitutional Law for Christian Students, Michael Farris, Home School Legal Defense Association
▸ Teacher helps: teacher's handbook with answers
▸ Description: A course on understanding the highest law of our land, the Constitution. Written by Mike Farris of the Home School Legal Defense Association, this course is available on-line. See HSLDA's Web site, www.hslda.org, for information.

ECONOMICS

| *Course:* **Remedial Economics** | *Grade:* **11-12** | *Prerequisite:* **American History** |

Biblical Economics in Comics, Vic Lockman
▸ Teacher helps: none needed
Whatever Happened to Penny Candy?, Bluestocking Press
▸ Teacher helps: study guide
▸ Description: *Biblical Economics* and *Penny Candy* present some economic basics in an easily understood and entertaining way. These two books will give the struggling student some understanding of economics on a very basic level.

ECONOMICS (CONT'D)

Course: **Economics**	*Grade:* **11-12**	*Prerequisite:* **U.S. & World Hist.**

Biblical Economics in Comics, Vic Lockman
▸ Teacher helps: none needed

Whatever Happened to Penny Candy?, Bluestocking Press
▸ Teacher helps: study guide

Economics in One Easy Lesson, Henry Hazlitt
▸ Teacher helps: no guide available

▸ Description: An interesting introduction to economics. *Biblical Economics* and *Penny Candy* present some basics in an easily understood and entertaining way. Once the student understands these basics, begin Hazlitt's book. It is a more scholarly but approachable explanation of economics. It would be an appropriate book to grade using chapter and book summarizations.

Course: **Economics**	*Grade:* **11-12**	*Prerequisite:* **U.S. & World Hist.**

Economics, Bob Jones University Press
▸ Teacher helps: teacher's edition, tests and key, teacher's edition for student activity book, *Testbuilder* software

▸ Description: This one semester course should be one of the last social studies taught in high school because of the more advanced reasoning that economics requires. Another beautiful full color hardbound book from Bob Jones University Press.

Course: **Advanced Economics**	*Grade:* **11-12**	*Prerequisite:* **U.S. & World Hist.**

Basic Economics, Clarence Carson, American Textbook Committee
▸ Teacher helps: none available

▸ Description: This course will present economics from a conservative viewpoint. Because of the independent nature of the course (no teacher guide is available) this may be most suited for advanced students with an interest in this area. However, we have always found Clarence Carson interesting and very readable. Chapter and book summaries would be an appropriate grading tool.

WORLDVIEW AND SOCIAL ISSUES

| *Course:* **Modern Philosophies** | *Grade:* **9-12** | *Prerequisite:* **American History** |

Understanding the Times, student abridged text and workbook, ACSI and Summit Ministries
▸ Teacher helps: teacher's guide
or *Understanding the Times* **tape series**, student fill-in notebooks, Summit Ministries
▸ Teacher helps: teacher's notebook
▸ Description: This worldview study contrasts the basic worldviews prevalent today with the Christian worldview. It is a helpful foundation and eye opener for any student, especially if he is going away from home to college. The forerunner to this program is the excellent, but expensive, video tape series available through Summit Ministries. (Perhaps a home school support group could purchase them cooperatively.) They provide an excellent filter through which to view the world. See Appendix A for Summit Ministries' address.

| *Course:* **Worldview Camps** | *Grade:* **9-12** | *Prerequisite:* **none** |

▸ Description: Summit Ministries operates a camp in Colorado where high school students can go for a two week study on the major worldviews. All are studied and evaluated in light of the Christian worldview. It is an intense time but good fun also. A similar organization, Worldview Academy, offers a one week camp. Worldview Academy will accept students a bit younger and is offered at different locations throughout the United States. My three oldest children have had the blessing of attending Worldview Academy. We consider it an essential for a high school education. Any time spent at Summit or Worldview Academy is time well spent. Check Appendix A for address information.

| *Course:* **Current Events** | *Grade:* **9-12** | *Prerequisite:* **none** |

WORLD **magazine**, God's World Publications
local newspaper
▸ Teacher helps: none available on this level
▸ Description: A current events course can be built on reading the local daily newspaper and the weekly news magazine, *World*. *World* is written from a Christian worldview. Call 1-800-951-6397 for ordering information.

| *Course:* **Independent Reading** (Current Events) | *Grade:* **9-12** | *Prerequisite:* **none** |

selected living books
▸ Teacher helps: none
▸ Description: An independent reading course is well-suited to a study of worldviews and how they relate to current issues and events. Plan an independent reading course using a variety of periodicals and books exploring current issues from a Christian perspective. Use a time record for evaluation. An opinion paper on an issue studied would be an appropriate requirement.

ADDITIONAL WORLDVIEW AND SOCIAL ISSUE TITLES

How Should We Then Live?, Francis Schaeffer
▶ Description: This book is subtitled *The Rise and Decline of Western Thought and Culture*. It is a survey of history showing how we have arrived at our twentieth century thinking. After reading the book, one can review by watching the video series of the same name.

How Now Shall We Live?, Charles Colson
▶ Description: Colson believes that the struggles of modern life are due to the many conflicting worldviews prevalent today. After a look at various scriptural themes, Colson makes pertinent applications to all areas of life.

Seven Men Who Rule the World from the Grave, David Breese
▶ Description: Learn about seven men whose ideas have had a profound effect on our world.

Angels in the Architecture, Doug Wilson
▶ Description: This thought-provoking book is a call to applying Christianity to every area of life using a medieval model as our example.

Postmodern Times, Gene Edward Veith
▶ Description: If you enjoy reading social issue books, this book provides an analysis of our world today. We have enjoyed Gene Veith's readable writing style.

State of the Arts, Gene Edward Veith
▶ Description: This book examines the arts and sets a standard for Christian evaluation.

The Road to Serfdom, F.A. Hayek
▶ Description: *The Road to Serfdom* deals with the relationship between individual freedom and economic prosperity. It builds a case against government interference and control of the market place.

The Law, Frederic Bastiat, Foundation for Economic Education
▶ Description: This little booklet was first published in 1850 by the French economist, Frederic Bastiat. His arguments against socialism are as pertinent today as they were when first written.

In the Shadow of Plenty, George Grant
▶ Description: A Christian response to poverty.

Compassionate Conservatism, Marvin Olasky
▶ Description: President George W. Bush's phrase "compassionate conservatism" is a testimony to the influence this book has had on his domestic policy ideas. A pertinent book to read at this time in our country's history.

High School and Unit Studies

Many home schoolers who have used unit studies in the elementary grades would like to continue to use them on the high school level. Is this possible?

Unit studies, sometimes called interdisciplinary studies, can be used on the high school level. In an interdisciplinary approach subjects are woven together using some unifying factor. Often a study is unified by historical time period, with history and English being very easy to combine in this manner. Many unit studies, especially for younger students, are woven around character qualities.

The key to using unit studies on the high school level is keeping records that can be effectively reported on a transcript. Often unit study authors provide the guidance you need. Some offer record keeping procedures and/or suggest the number of credits a student can earn following their program.

When designing your own unit study, you can keep separate records for each subject being studied. For example, a historical study can be divided into three time records, one each for English (literature and composition), history, and government.

If you plan to follow a portfolio approach to record keeping you probably won't feel the need to separate your unit study into separate courses. It also may not be necessary when applying to a smaller college with more individualized admission practices. Always use the approach most helpful to the future of your student.

If unit studies appeal to you, you may want to check into the following high school studies:

1. *History of the World* by Konos is a two volume study of world history. Volume One is titled "The Ancient World," with Volume Two covering "The Medieval World." History, English, art, geography, and Bible are all integrated into the study. See www.konos.com for information.

2. The Cornerstone Curriculum Project publishes a three year unit study recommended for grades eight through twelve. Entitled *Worldviews of the Western World,* it covers ancient through modern history. This program features the works of Dr. Francis Schaeffer and is very intellectually challenging. CCP also has math, art, and music courses. See www.cornerstonecurriculum.com for more information.

3. *Where the Brook and River Meet* by Margie Gray is a unit study on the Victorian Era based on Lucy Maude Montgomery's *Anne of Green Gables*. More information on this program can be obtained from www.CadronCreek.com.

4. Sonlight Curriculum is a living book unit study. A visit to www.sonlightcurriculum.com provides information on their ninth grade program, "20th Century World History," and their 10th grade "Civics/Government" and "American Literature."

What about Computer Courses?

Computers may seem beyond our capability as parents, but they never seem to intimidate children. The best way to learn to use a computer is — to use a computer.

Although using a computer is a wonderful technological help, there are some cautions, particularly regarding unrestricted use of the Internet or chat rooms. Although many marvelous things exist on the net, so do new depths of depravity. Be wise and aware. Guard the hearts and minds of your children.

I will not be recommending any particular courses for computer use, just making a few suggestions.

Always teach proper use of the keyboard first. It is likely that by high school your teen already has been taught to use the keyboard properly or has developed his own "hunt and peck style." Habits are hard to break, but it would be to your student's advantage to learn the proper way to type. Mavis Beacon's course is just one of the programs available to teach this skill.

Once they can type properly, teach your students how to use the word processing program on your computer and any other software that is in frequent use on your home computer (games excluded!). Other possible resources for learning computer skills would be continuing education classes or classes for credit at the junior college and courses offered by computer stores.

If you do not have a computer, you may want to consider making the purchase. If your student is going to college, word processing skills will be vitally important.

FOREIGN LANGUAGE COURSES

Learning a foreign language is achievable at home. There are many self-teaching cassette programs available. Often these programs are directed towards the traveler needing quick exposure to the language he will soon encounter. This type of approach will emphasize a quick immersion in words of greatest need while traveling. It will be helpful for the student taking a mission's trip, but does not provide the thoroughness of a high school language program.

There are two basic instructional approaches to teaching a foreign language. They are immersion programs or traditional grammatical language studies.

The first priority of an immersion program is learning to converse in the language fluently. Grammar is de-emphasized, with grammatical concepts introduced bit by bit when necessary for further growth in the language. Language immersion is the way we learned our native language as babies and small children.

When using an immersion program be sure that the tapes or CD's presenting the information have accurate and clear pronunciation. Then have reasonable expectations. Foreign language studies will be much more effective if the student has daily opportunities to use the language. For example, living here in Texas, there are many opportunities for hearing and speaking Spanish. Short term missionary service is another possibility. Along with its spiritual benefits, it can also provide instant and complete language immersion. Remember fluency in our native language did not happen quickly, but occurred over many years of childhood. Fluency in a new language won't occur overnight for teens either!

A more traditional approach to language studies begins with an emphasis on the structure of the language. Grammar is studied as the cohesive foundation underlying the language. Students will memorize lists of declensions and conjugations, applying these grammatical structures to the vocabulary learned. Translation work from English into the foreign language and from the foreign language into English will be completed. If the language is spoken today, there will also be an emphasis on clear pronunciation via tapes and CD's.

Both approaches will usually contain information on the culture, land, history, and people.

Which way is best? That depends on your goals. If fluency is most important, consider an immersion program (while hopefully not neglecting grammar). If the main goal is learning to read and write in a classical, unspoken language, a traditional approach seems most helpful. The following box discusses the value of studying Latin. Finally, if total mastery of the language is the goal, then immersion and grammar are both necessary.

Why Teach Latin?

Teaching Latin is one of the things we did right in our home school. Unfortunately, it took us three years with three different programs to find the right approach. With that finally settled, we began to see both expected and unexpected benefits.

We expected to see vocabulary improvement. Studies confirm that studying Latin improves SAT scores. However, studying Latin roots may accomplish that without the extra work of studying Latin as a language. It was the unexpected benefits that convinced us of Latin's importance in our home school.

We had not expected the study of English grammar to finally acquire purpose and meaning. Translation work requires an understanding of parts of speech, noun functions, verb tenses, etc. Now there was a reason to remember all those tedious details — we were using them with meaning. They became vital clues to the translation puzzles we were continually solving.

We had not expected Latin to teach us how to think. In math, geometry teaches logical thought processes through formal proofs. When studying an inflected language, such as Latin, a similar exercise in careful, methodical thought takes place. Accurate translation work requires orderly thought. If orderly thinking becomes habitual, it will be a lifelong advantage.

FOREIGN LANGUAGE

| *Course:* **Foreign Language** | *Grade:* **all grades** | *Prerequisite:* **none** |

Smart Start, Syracuse Language
▸ Teacher helps: none needed
▸ Description: Use this CD-Rom interactive program to build pronunciation, vocabulary, and conversational skills. Some grammar included. Consider it a supplement to your foreign language program. Available in Spanish, German, Italian, and French.

| *Course:* **Foreign Language I and II** | *Grade:* **9-12** | *Prerequisite:* **none** |

Powerglide Spanish, German, French, Latin, Russian, or *Japanese* workbook and tapes or CDs
▸ Teacher helps: learner's guide, tests, listening tape
▸ Description: *Powerglide* language courses are nontraditional courses which quickly immerse your student in the language being studied. If the program is successfully completed, your student has completed the equivalent of at least two years of high school foreign language. Originally on tapes only, *Powerglide* is moving into a CD presentation.

| *Course:* **Spanish I** | *Grade:* **9-12** | *Prerequisite:* **none** |

Spanish, Alpha-Omega
▸ Teacher helps: teacher's manual, tapes
▸ Description: This is a self-paced worktext audio tape program. It has been very recently revised and improved. Gaining familiarity with the language through conversation is emphasized.

| *Course:* **Spanish II** | *Grade:* **9-12** | *Prerequisite:* **Spanish I** |

Spanish II, Alpha-Omega
▸ Teacher helps: teacher's manual, tapes
▸ Description: *Spanish II* is a brand new 2001 product. It is a self-paced worktext audio tape program. This second level is an intensive grammar study built upon the vocabulary skills learned in *Spanish I.*

| *Course:* **Spanish I & II** | *Grade:* **9-12** | *Prerequisite:* **none** |

Spanish I & II, Bob Jones University Press
Spanish I & II Student Activities Books, Bob Jones University Press
▸ Teacher helps: teacher's edition, teacher edition's for student activity books, cassettes, video supplements, tests and keys
▸ Description: The Bob Jones University Press Spanish courses require a teacher with knowledge in the foreign language. However, with the use of BJUP's HomeSat program, this program should become usable to more home schoolers. Both Spanish I and II are available on HomeSat.

FOREIGN LANGUAGE (CONT'D)

Course: Spanish III   Grade: **9-12**   Prerequisite: **none**

Spanish Three Years, Bob Jones University Press
▸ Teacher helps: answer key
Momentos Hispanos, available through Bob Jones University Press Catalog
▸ Teacher helps: answer key
Historia de la Biblia, available through Bob Jones University Press Catalog
▸ Teacher helps: none needed
▸ Description: Bob Jones University Press has recently added Spanish III to their HomeSat program. A new course, it does not have the same hardback text presentation of Spanish I and II. Contact BJUP's HomeSat for more information.

Course: French I & II   Grade: **9-12**   Prerequisite: **none**

French I & II, Bob Jones University Press
French I and II Student Activities Books, Bob Jones University Press
▸ Teacher helps: teacher's edition, teacher edition's for student activity books, cassettes, video supplement for *French I*, tests and keys
▸ Description: The BJUP French courses require a teacher with knowledge in the foreign language. However, with the use of their HomeSat program, this program should become usable to more home schoolers. HomeSat carries both French I and II.

Course: Latin I   Grade: **9-12**   Prerequisite: **none**

Latin I, Bob Jones University Press
Latin I Student Activities Book, Bob Jones University Press
▸ Teacher helps: teacher's edition, teacher edition's for student activity book, tests and key
▸ Description: This recently added BJUP language program does not require a teacher with knowledge in the foreign language. It is not available on HomeSat.

Course: Latin I-III   Grade: **9-12**   Prerequisite: **none**

The Latin Road to English Grammar I-III student workbooks, Schola
▸ Teacher helps: includes teacher's manual, pronunciation tape, tests
▸ Description: This is an excellent program marketed to home schoolers. Parents without a Latin background can teach this text if they are willing to learn along with their students. Each year's text covers a full year's language instruction, but you may desire to supplement with readings on the Roman culture. Available in three levels: Latin I, Latin II, and Latin III.

FINE ARTS COURSES

The fine arts are often neglected, but that need not happen. Here are a few suggestions.

Having your student home all day makes it easy to expose him to classical music. Consider allowing the quiet playing of classical music during study time. Watch your local paper for classical or high quality concerts in the area. Sometimes these concerts have no admission charge.

Many students complain about music lessons. We consider piano lessons an expected part of school, no different than English, math, or history. Home schooling allows practice time to blend into the school day.

Art can often be enjoyed through group art lessons offered in a home school support group or local art and craft stores. When traveling, consider adding art museums to your sight-seeing plans. Some helpful resources for fine arts appreciation are available through various home school catalogs.

Art courses can be graded or credited based on the overall direction of the course. Evaluation of a music or art appreciation course, with reading and listening requirements, could be based on time spent. Project courses could be based on the completion of contracted activities, with a time record kept if needed.

The first suggested fine arts course is speech. Speech would be a good group course so students have an audience for presentations. Consider taking it in eleventh or twelfth grade so the student has learned or is learning the necessary composition skills. Or if you desire to keep a time record, you could work on this course over all four years of high school, doing memorized presentations of other's work and progressing to original speeches as composition skills mature.

Speech is a course that is hard to categorize. I have followed our state's lead and placed it in fine arts. Should your state credit speech as an English course, you should credit it as an English course also.

SPEECH

| *Course:* **Speech** | *Grade:* **11-12** | *Prerequisite:* **none** |

On Speaking Well, Peggy Noonan
▸ Teacher helps: none
▸ Description: Peggy Noonan is best remembered as President Reagan's speech writer. This pithy little book gives excellent help in preparing and delivering winning speeches. Interesting anecdotal information from her career often illustrates her points. Written for adults, it would be most appropriate for older high school students.

| *Course:* **Speech** | *Grade:* **9-12** | *Prerequisite:* **none** |

Speech **worktexts**, School of Tomorrow
▸ Teacher helps: answer keys
▸ Description: This is a half year course that uses six worktexts (paces) to teach the basics of effective speech.

| *Course:* **Speech** | *Grade:* **10-12** | *Prerequisite:* **none** |

Speech, Bob Jones University Press
▸ Teacher helps: teacher's edition
▸ Description: Speech topics covered include vocal production, preparing and delivering different types of speeches, debate, parliamentary procedure, and oral interpretation of poetry, stories, and plays.

MUSIC

| *Course:* **Music** | *Grade:* **9-12** | *Prerequisite:* **none** |

assigned by teacher
▸ Description: Consider any private lessons as a high school music course.

| *Course:* **Music Appreciation** | *Grade:* **9-12** | *Prerequisite:* **none** |

The Spiritual Lives of the Great Composers, Patrick Kavanaugh
▸ Teacher helps: none needed
▸ Description: An introduction to classical music and its composers. Reading *The Spiritual Lives of the Great Composers* and its vignettes on various composers is as spiritually edifying as it is informative. Each vignette concludes with thoughts on a particular godly quality that was outstanding in that composer. Listening recommendations for each composer are also given. Fortunately, classical music is often very reasonably priced, and it is not difficult to build a good listening library. Should your student desire to delve more deeply into each composer's life, *The Gift of Music* by Jane Stuart Smith and Betty Carlson gives additional information. This book is also from a Christian perspective.

ART

Course: **Art Appreciation**	*Grade:* **9-12**	*Prerequisite:* **none**

Annotated Art, Cumming/Dorling Kindersley
Annotated Mona Lisa, Carol Strickland
History of Art for Young People, H. W. Jansen
The Story of Painting, Sister Wendy Beckett
▸ Teacher helps: none needed
▸ Description: Full color pictorial walks through art history with helpful commentary along the way. Jansen's and Sister Wendy's volumes are much larger, more thorough volumes. As with any art books, expect some nudity.

Course: **Art & Crafts**	*Grade:* **9-12**	*Prerequisite:* **none**

assigned by teacher
▸ Description: This would be a project course using classes or materials offered in your community or craft store.

Course: **Art — Drawing**	*Grade:* **9-12**	*Prerequisite:* **none**

Mark Kistler's Draw Squad, Mark Kistler
▸ Teacher helps: none needed
▸ Description: Skill sequenced, step-by-step lessons build a student's drawing skills through daily practice. Kistler's "ten key words of drawing" explain how to make drawings appear three-dimensional. Although this book is targeted towards younger children, its drawing instruction makes it helpful for any novice. Mark Kistler has several other books geared for younger children which may be adaptable for older students.

Course: **Art — Drawing**	*Grade:* **9-12**	*Prerequisite:* **none**

Draw Today, Walter Foster
▸ Teacher helps: nothing additional needed
▸ Description: A drawing course with materials and demonstration video included. Walter Foster has other art kits often available at arts and crafts stores.

Course: **Cartooning**	*Grade:* **9-12**	*Prerequisite:* **none**

The Big Book of Cartooning I & II, Vic Lockman
▸ Teacher helps: none needed
▸ Description: An independent, hands-on study of cartooning.

Course: **Calligraphy**	*Grade:* **9-12**	*Prerequisite:* **none**

check local arts and crafts store
▸ Teacher helps: none needed
▸ Description: Check your local arts and crafts store for possible classes and materials.

Course: **Art**	*Grade:* **7-12**	*Prerequisite:* **none**

Art Lifepacs 1-10, Alpha Omega
▸ Teacher helps: teacher's guide
▸ Description: This worktext program covers a wide variety of topics including design, color, perspective, figure drawing, sculpture, comics, printmaking, calligraphy, and art appreciation.

P.E. AND HEALTH COURSES

As Christians, we have a responsibility to take care of the bodies God has given us. The study of health and the pursuit of some type of physical activity help meet that responsibility.

The study of health, because it involves lifestyle choices, can include significant spiritual discussion. It can also become a course which contains all kinds of questionable content. Teaching health at home allows you to choose what topics to study and lets you study them in a way that harmonizes with your family values. Three textbook options from a Christian perspective are suggested. Living books on health and nutrition, dating or courtship, and marriage and family living can also be incorporated into a health curriculum.

Physical education is often neglected in home schooling. Many child development specialists believe that the higher level thinking skills are built upon well-functioning motor skills. Walking, jogging, playing ball, swimming, tennis, etc. may actually help academic performance.

P. E. AND HEALTH

| *Course:* **Physical Education** | *Grade:* **9-12** | *Prerequisite:* **none** |

▸ Description: Activities designed to teach a physical skill or improve physical fitness. Some possibilities for completing this requirement include church or community sport leagues, continuing education courses at the junior college, health club memberships, or individual fitness plans.

| *Course:* **Health** | *Grade:* **7-12** | *Prerequisite:* **none** |

General Health Lifepac Select, Alpha Omega

▸ Teacher helps: teacher's guide

▸ Description: Alpha Omega *Select* electives are lifepacs topically chosen to create a one semester course.

| *Course:* **Health** | *Grade:* **9-12** | *Prerequisite:* **none** |

Health worktexts, School of Tomorrow

▸ Teacher helps: answer keys

▸ Description: Because of the sensitive nature of many health topics, it is wise to stay with health texts from a Christian perspective. This program meets that requirement with an easy worktext format.

| *Course:* **Health** | *Grade:* **9-12** | *Prerequisite:* **none** |

Health, Bob Jones University Press

▸ Teacher helps: teacher's edition, tests on two difficulty levels, blackline masters

▸ Description: Because Bob Jones recommends this text for use in seventh grade and above they have produced two levels of tests. They have also placed the most sensitive topics in blackline masters, rather than the text, so these topics can be added at the teacher or parent's discretion.

HOME ECONOMICS COURSES

With the focus of our world removed from the home, home economics often becomes an underemphasized area of study. Yet courses such as these help build the refuge every person needs from the stresses and strains of the world. Both men and women alike need to know how to create and maintain that refuge from day to day. Many living books which help in these studies are available in Christian bookstores.

For young women there are almost endless possibilities for study. Anything that teaches the Biblical role of a woman, nurture of a family, and comfort of a home is a fair course topic. When planning, don't forget your own areas of talent that you can teach your teen. What we have offered here are only a few suggestions — how about gardening, canning and preserving, housecleaning, home decorating, etc. for additional possibilities?

For young men the possibilities for study are also extensive. Personal survival skills such as basic cooking, cleaning, and sewing skills are helpful. For future family life, books on male leadership, marriage relationships, and parenting would be appropriate. Courses on money management, home maintenance, car repair, and carpentry skills would all be an asset.

Both young men and women would benefit from a study on courtship and dating. Several book suggestions are included in the Bible and character course section earlier in this book.

For course evaluation, a course contract which establishes reading and activity goals would be appropriate. This could be combined with a time record, if desired, to insure that sufficient time is spent to justify the credit awarded.

HOME ECONOMICS/AUTO MAINTENANCE

Course: **Cooking and Nutrition** Grade: **9-12** *Prerequisite:* **none**

Use cookbooks and nutritional information from home or the library.
‣ Teacher helps: not needed
‣ Description: Make this a practical hands-on course. Study nutrition, plan nutritionally balanced menus, shop, and prepare meals. You determine the exact goals.

Course: **Child Care** Grade: **9-12** *Prerequisite:* **none**

Shepherding a Child's Heart, Tedd Tripp
‣ Teacher helps: Application questions at the end of each chapter.
a pediatric CPR course, check with your local Red Cross
‣ Description: A course combining Christian childrearing and safety. Evaluation could include some free baby sitting for a friend so your teen can practice her improving skills under your supervision.

Course: **Family Living** Grade: **9-12** *Prerequisite:* **none**

Choose from:
Christian Living in the Home, Jay Adams
The Shaping of a Christian Home, Elisabeth Elliot
Hidden Art, Edith Schaeffer
What is a Family?, Edith Schaeffer
‣ Teacher helps: none available
‣ Description: A course with an emphasis on relationships in the home.

Course: **Handwork** Grade: **9-12** *Prerequisite:* **none**

any "how to" book from a local craft store.
‣ Description: A practical hands-on course in various types of handwork — you choose. Choices could include counted cross stitch, quilting, knitting, crocheting, etc. If mom doesn't have the skills to teach this course, grandmother, a friend, or a course at a local sewing or craft store may do nicely.

Course: **Garment Construction** Grade: **9-12** *Prerequisite:* **none**

‣ Teacher helps: pattern, sewing reference book of your choice
‣ Description: A project course. I sewed my first garments with the help of my retired great aunt. It is a wonderful memory.

Course: **Economic Living**   *Grade:* **9-12**   *Prerequisite:* **none**

Possible Choices:

More with Less Cookbook, Doris Longacre

Tightwad Gazette I, II, or III, Amy Dacyczyn

▶ Description: A course teaching the student money-saving tips and how to cook economically. Implementing some of the money-saving ideas learned in these books in your home could be a course requirement. Other possible resources could be: *Once a Month Cooking, Dinner's in the Freezer*, or *More with Less Living*. Check your County Agricultural Extension Service (or similar state organization) for free publications.

Course: **Home Economics**   *Grade:* **9-12**   *Prerequisite:* **none**

Home Economics Lifepacs 1-10, Alpha Omega

▶ Teacher helps: teacher's guide

▶ Description: This is a worktext program covering all the major topics in a home economics course written from a Christian perspective.

Course: **Home/Auto Maintenance**   *Grade:* **9-12**   *Prerequisite:* **none**

anything the parent finds useful.

▶ Description: A practical course where the student works with his mother or father in routine home and car maintenance. Grant credits based on time spent.

THINKING/STUDY SKILLS/CAREER

There are a few final areas of study to consider. They are thinking skills, study skills, and career exploration. We will look at each area briefly.

Materials for sharpening figural and verbal thinking skills are listed first. Formal logic materials from two publishers popular on the home school market follow these general thinking skill recommendations. We all think, but most of us have not been formally trained to think logically!

Next, materials for developing good study skills are given. Success at the college level depends as much (or more!) on organizational skills and carefully cultivated study habits as it does on natural ability. Therefore, a video course for improving general study habits is included. A few products popular with home schoolers are suggested for college entrance test preparation. However, don't stop with these suggestions. A thoughtful browse through almost any bookstore will provide you with many possibilities. Again, Cathy Duffy and Mary Pride's books review the features of many popular college test preparation materials.

Finally, materials for career exploration are recommended. The first suggestion comes from a Christian perspective, making it especially helpful for the Christian young person seeking God's will.

THINKING/STUDY SKILL/CAREER COURSES

| *Course:* **Thinking Skills** | *Grade:* **10-12** | *Prerequisite:* **none** |

Building Thinking Skills, Book 3: Figural, Critical Thinking Press
Building Thinking Skills, Book 3: Verbal, Critical Thinking Press
  ▸ Teacher helps: separate teacher's manual for each
  ▸ Description: A course geared to developing thinking skills helpful for improving overall academic performance.

| *Course:* **Logic** | *Grade:* **9-12** | *Prerequisite:* **none** |

Traditional Logic I & II, Martin Cothran/Memoria Press
  ▸ Teacher helps: answer key included
  ▸ Description: I have reviewed a lot of materials on logic from my nonexpert, but helpful perspective — that of a parent who feels totally incompetent to teach the subject. This is the first program that gives me hope! Mr. Cothran's writing style is easy to understand. His assignments for mastering the material are easy to follow. If you survive the first level, a second level awaits you.

| *Course:* **Logic** | *Grade:* **8 and up** | *Prerequisite:* **none** |

Introductory Logic, Douglas Wilson and James Nance, Canon Press
  ▸ Teacher helps: solution key, video set
  ▸ Description: This introductory logic course now has a video set available which teaches the student the skills presented in the textbook.

| *Course:* **Logic II** | *Grade:* **8 and up** | *Prerequisite:* **none** |

Intermediate Logic, Douglas Wilson and James Nance, Canon Press
  ▸ Teacher helps: solution key, video set
  ▸ Description: This intermediate logic course now has a video set available which teaches the student the skills presented in the textbook.

| *Course:* **Study Skills** | *Grade:* **9-12** | *Prerequisite:* **none** |

How to be a Superstar Student, The Teaching Company
  ▸ Teacher helps: none required
  ▸ Description: This two video set is a course on how to study with the goal of college success. Watching this course early in the student's high school years will give him four years to practice the techniques taught before beginning college. Tim McGee, the video instructor, is both a coach and an English teacher. This unusual combination results in a lively presentation style with many sports illustrations. This is a plus for male viewers but should not be a problem to unathletic viewers. See Appendix A for address information.

| *Course:* **SAT Preparation** | *Grade:* **7-12** | *Prerequisite:* **none** |

Analogies 1, **2**, and **3**, Educator's Publishing Service
▸ Teacher helps: answers in back of book
▸ Description: Studying analogies improves reasoning ability and critical thinking. *Analogies 1, 2, & 3* get progressively more difficult, with decreasing explanation given. EPS has given us a helpful addition to SAT preparation.

| *Course:* **SAT Preparation** | *Grade:* **9-12** | *Prerequisite:* **none** |

SAT Math Review, Chalk Dust Company
▸ Teacher helps: none needed
▸ Description: A series of five videos brings the student through the algebra and geometry skills necessary for success on the SAT college entrance exam.

| *Course:* **SAT Preparation** | *Grade:* **9-12** | *Prerequisite:* **none** |

The Princeton Review: Inside the SAT, ACT & PSAT, The Learning Company
▸ Teacher helps: none needed
▸ Description: A CD-ROM program providing a step-by-step method for preparing for college entrance tests.

| *Course:* **College Planning** | *Grade:* **9-12** | *Prerequisite:* **none** |

Switched on Schoolhouse College Planner, Alpha Omega
▸ Teacher helps: none needed
▸ Description: A one semester computerized course that helps students with college planning, selection, and application.

| *Course:* **Career Exploration** | *Grade:* **9-12** | *Prerequisite:* **none** |

Career Net, Life Pathways, Crown Financial Ministries
▸ Teacher helps: student-directed program
▸ Description: *Career Net Guidance System's* various components help the Christian young person discover God's direction for his life. The student begins by filling out a questionnaire. He then listens to several audio messages before working through the Career Direct assessment CD-ROM program. After printing out the assessment results the student listens to several more audio tapes, develops an action plan, and evaluates different potential occupations. When finished, the student should have a realistic picture for formulating future goals.

| *Course:* **Career Exploration** | *Grade:* **9-12** | *Prerequisite:* **none** |

What Color is Your Parachute?, Richard Nelson Bolles, Ten Speed Press
▸ Teacher helps: none required
▸ Description: *What Color is Your Parachute?,* as its cover proclaims, is the best selling job-hunting book in the world. It is well worth a look. Because of its popularity you should be able to find it at your library.

Earning College Credit

Is your student interested in getting an early start on college? If so, there are several different ways to accomplish that goal.

One possibility is earning college credit through dual/concurrent enrollment programs at junior or community colleges. Another means is testing. The College Board has two different testing programs that can help your student earn advanced college placement or early college credit. They are the Advanced Placement exams (AP exams) and College Level Examination Program (CLEP exams). Let's look briefly at all three options.

Early College Enrollment

Many home schoolers begin their college studies under a dual/concurrent enrollment agreement with a local junior or community college. Courses which count towards both high school and college credit are taken on campus. Sometimes there are Internet course options. Policies and procedures will change from school to school. To avoid misunderstandings and potential disappointment research school policies carefully.

Advantages to Early College Enrollment

1   Difficult lab science or math courses can be taken at the junior college. This provides good instruction for the student and relieves the parent of a substantial preparation burden.

2.   General college study requirements can be fulfilled earlier.

3.   Students can get a taste of college before leaving home.

Disadvantages to Early College Enrollment

1.   Earning college credits can affect a student's freshman standing when applying to four year institutions. This may disqualify your student for scholarships offered only to four year students.

2.   Sometimes college credit is held until the student has completed high school. After graduation these credits are released and added to his transcript.

3.   When transferring, it is possible that a college could refuse to grant college credit for a course that also received high school credit.

4.   Taking college courses at a younger age may expose home school students to issues and situations they are not yet prepared to handle. If this is a concern, check to see if your local junior or community college offers any classes via the Internet.

ADVANCED PLACEMENT EXAMS

AP, or Advanced Placement exams are taken by high school students to earn advanced placement in college. Examples of some of the exams available include biology, English, Spanish, and U.S. history. Public high schools often offer advanced placement classes for students that culminate in taking the AP exam. Thanks to the home business PA Homeschoolers (www.pahomeschoolers.com) AP preparation courses are also available to home schoolers nationwide. Although other on-line services exist, PA Homeschoolers prices may fit the home school pocketbook better.

Advantages to Advanced Placement Exams

1. The College Board offers the Scholar Award recognition program for students reaching noteworthy levels of achievement using AP exams. Although not a monetary program, it can lead to increased financial offerings from college aid plans.

2. An ambitious student who successfully completes a number of AP exams can actually begin college with a sophomore standing.

3. Less ambitious testing plans can still enhance your student's chances of being accepted at more competitive colleges, perhaps with scholarship money included.

4. Your student can experience college level work without leaving home.

Disadvantages to Advanced Placement Exams

1. AP exams do not necessarily replace college level *credits*. Testing out of courses does not automatically mean the student will receive credit for those courses; it may only mean that they bypass early level college courses and advance directly into more advanced courses.

2. Colleges make their own decisions about how to handle AP exams. This means you must research carefully to avoid false expectations. Check Web sites or college catalogs for policies.

3. AP exams are offered on high school campuses. School personnel are not always eager to accommodate home schoolers in their testing situations.

4. AP exams are offered only in May. This means senior year AP exams will not be completed in time to appear on most transcripts.

CLEP EXAMS

The College Level Examination Program can help students earn college credit for examinations successfully completed. CLEP exams take two forms: general and subject.

Six general examinations cover wide subject areas. They are English composition, college mathematics, humanities, natural science, and social sciences and history. Satisfactory completion of these tests can result in three to six college credit hours.

Subject area tests correspond to individual college courses with similar titles. Examples of subject area tests include American government, introduction to psychology, college algebra, and general biology.

Advantages to CLEP Exams

1. They provide a means for home school high schoolers to begin earning college credit.

2. They allow the student to get general study requirements completed quickly so they can move into course work in their major field of study.

3. CLEP exams are very reasonably priced. This potentially saves the student a substantial amount of money over the course of a four year college program.

Disadvantages to CLEP Exams

1. Colleges will only award CLEP credit to students enrolled in their academic program.

2. Each college decides which CLEP tests they will accept. Some accept a wide variety, others significantly limit the CLEP tests they will accept. "Clepping" without complete knowledge can lead to disappointment and frustration. Check individual college Web sites or catalogs for policies.

3. Taking CLEP tests in the student's major area of study can be an inferior learning experience to the interaction of the live classroom.

Final Note

If testing options appeal to you, test preparation materials are usually stocked or can be special ordered from any large bookstore. In addition, visit the College Board's excellent Web site, www.collegeboard.org, for information on both the AP and CLEP exam programs. Information on the PSAT/NMSQT, SAT I, and SAT II exams is also available. Their on-line store also offers study materials for purchase.

Are There New Options for Earning a College Degree?

Although it has been possible to earn an advanced degree by correspondence for many years, the distance learning choices are increasing. With the new technology available through the Internet, this trend should continue to grow. However, any time a new field opens businesses can spring up rapidly. Not all will be reputable. It is no different with distance learning.

It is very important that you research all schools offering degrees by correspondence carefully. Dr. John Bear has been researching these schools for years. *Bear's Guide to Earning Degrees by Distance Learning* is a large volume, with a comprehensive selection of programs. *College Degrees by Mail and Internet,* also by Bear, reviews only the correspondence schools he considers especially praiseworthy. Jason D. Baker's book, *Baker's Guide to Christian Distance Education* may also prove helpful to you. Three more options are Peterson's *The Independent Study Catalog,* Sam Atieh's *How To Get a College Degree Via the Internet,* and Kevin Paul's *Get Your University Degree at Home.* A visit to a large bookstore may reveal even more choices.

If you are particularly interested in distance learning via the Internet, there are a number of Web sites that can give you more information. Baker's Guide to Christian Distance Learning, www.gospelcom.net/bakersguide/, lists distance learning programs from Christian schools. Secular sites to check are www.geteducated.com and www.petersons.com. As mentioned above, check the credentials of a distance learning program carefully before enrolling.

One distance learning program that is presently getting some home school attention is the LionHawk program, a joint venture between Pennsylvania State University and Iowa State University. Students receiving a Letters, Arts, & Science Associates Degree (2LAS) from Penn State are accepted into Iowa's Bachelor of Liberal Studies (BLS) degree program. There are no residency requirements. Students successfully completing the programs receive the same diploma as students in their on-campus programs. Check their Web sites, www.worldcampus.psu.edu and www.uiowa.edu, for more information.

Part Four

Reflecting on the Journey

REFLECTING ON THE JOURNEY

As we come to the end of this book, your mind may be spinning with all the information we have covered together. I know that at times it has probably been a bit overwhelming. So it seems appropriate to change direction and share a few quiet thoughts. Although your high school journey may be just beginning, ours will soon be completed for a third time. Let me share a few reflections on what we have learned.

SPIRITUAL LESSONS

Many success stories float around home school circles. It's easy as a home school parent to feel that every home school family except yours has students who love learning, are behaviorally flawless, run successful home businesses, are National Merit Scholar finalists, and defer to mom and dad for every important decision in life. Without stepping into another home schooler's home, I can assure you on the best authority, the Word of God, that such perfect home school households do not exist.

First of all, the Bible makes it clear that we are all sinners. Rather than being a demoralizing reminder, it's a guilt-relieving doctrine. This truth makes us realize that home schooling does not create perfect homes, perfect parents, or perfect children. That is the life work of Jesus Christ. And while home schooling can contribute greatly to nurturing our children in the Lord, it doesn't cause the problem of sin to disappear. In fact, as we live closely with each other, sometimes it seems that our sin abounds! Despite our great desire, we cannot home school the sin nature out of our children. Our sin struggles, both child and parent alike, are our daily reminder of how greatly we need the Lord Jesus and his sacrifice.

Therefore, keep your home schooling in perspective. A God-honoring home schooled upbringing is a wonderful gift to any child, but don't tarnish your efforts by placing expectations on your home schooling that only God can fulfill.

Secondly, all problems are not handled easily. Since we still have younger children, I often pause to appreciate the blessing of problems that can be solved with a kiss and a rock in the rocking chair. A teen's life is not so simple. Helping him solve problems often means a willingness to listen, and listen for a long time, when you would rather be doing something else. God will bless you for pausing in your activities to make eye contact and listen with both ears.

Thirdly, when we hand our high schoolers their diploma, they are not finished products. Yet, as home school parents, we sometimes expect them to be. We can find ourselves on a roller coaster of emotions. The right decisions our children make can leave us in triumph, justified in our labor of love. Unfortunately, every wrong decision can leave us wondering how they could forget the lessons we worked so hard to put in them.

Sometimes it comes as a shock to realize our teens are autonomous individuals. Surprise! All of those years of home schooling may not have produced a mom or dad clone. Our teen's thoughts and actions are his own. Sometimes those thoughts and actions will carry a clear stamp of his upbringing; sometimes they will not. Just as we learned some of life's lessons the hard way to the dismay of our parents, so will our teens.

Remember, God's work of sanctification unfolds in a Christian over a lifetime, and a newly graduated home schooler is continuing in that process, not completing it. We must give our children the same opportunity to grow in grace that God gives us. Every decision they make will not be wise, any more than all of our decisions as parents are seasoned with wisdom. Let a realization of this truth sow patience as we view the imperfections of our shared humanity.

Finally, it is hard letting go. As home schoolers, we have kept our children more closely by our side than most parents. The growth in independence that begins gradually when most children are dropped off at the kindergarten door can hit us almost overnight as our high schooler finishes his home school program. Despite after-school jobs, summer camps, and other wing-testing opportunities, the break can be more sudden for home school parents.

As our children become adults, in a very real sense we return our caretaker responsibilities to God. If our teen is a Christian, we have confidence that God loves him perfectly and completely. We know He watches over him more diligently than we ever could and that His powers of influence have unsurpassed strength. We don't know what the future holds for our teen, nor has God chosen to reveal all the details to us. Part of our growth in grace is trusting Him just the same.

COLLEGE LESSONS

With two students in college we have also learned some lessons in this area.

First of all, junior or community college is a good place for the undecided student to begin. When future plans are subject to frequent change, it is helpful to avoid the large debts of a university education. Our children have been able to finance their community college education with part time jobs.

Secondly, academic scholarships aren't always the pot of gold at the end of the rainbow. Our oldest son attends a well-respected engineering school thanks to sizable scholarship awards, some of them merit based. Although we are very grateful for the financial help, there are some hidden catches to merit based money that I would like to share.

Keeping merit based scholarships can put a student under tremendous pressure. Every grade in every course gains an unreasonable significance. Sometimes the struggle to keep every grade high can take away much of the pleasure of learning. In time, the student learns to play the academic game. Various people have shared the following strategies with me:

1. Balance course loads each semester with a mixture of easy and hard courses.

2. Concentrate on the courses that have the most potential for improvement. A "B" turned into an "A" gains a grade point.

3. Drop classes that earn less than the needed grade. Stay in the course as long as possible to learn as much as possible, then drop it to retake, hopefully with a better grade, later. (Unless the class is an elective — then get out quickly and never return!) Caution: don't use this strategy too often or it can delay graduation!

4. If you despair of ever getting more than an average grade in a course, get approval to take it elsewhere. This strategy only works at schools where courses transferred in are not included in the GPA calculation or the transferred classes are significantly easier than their counterparts at the four year university.

5. Be wary of taking advanced courses when a standard level course is acceptable. A standard level course will satisfy the graduation plan without risking the GPA.

6. Listen to the opinion of other students. This information from the trenches can help you find the best teachers and determine the overall difficulty of a course in advance.

7. When possible, try to mix courses that base final grades on papers and those that require final exams. Papers can be worked on and finished during the semester, thus relieving the end of the semester test-studying crunch.

It can be difficult to play this academic game after a home school lifestyle that was based on encouraging learning for its own sake, not for the grades it produced. Unfortunately, the necessity of keeping merit scholarships is a hard fact of reality for many students. After an uncomfortable year adjusting, we have now learned to play the game, too.

While it may be necessary to play the game today, I am thankful that learning does not end with a college diploma. Learning will continue for a lifetime, through both the rewards of professional growth and the simple pleasure of pursuing personal interests.

FINAL THOUGHTS

Many home school books are liberally sprinkled with anecdotal information about the author's home school life. Home schooling can create anxiety. To combat those feelings, some writers may choose a chatty writing style to both comfort and build confidence in their reader. I have chosen a different approach. As a person who likes to get to the point quickly, I desired to keep the information streamlined and easy to locate for those moments when panic strikes. Consider it a 911 style of delivering information!

A second reason motivates me to limit anecdotal information. My husband has been a pastor for approximately twenty years. We have also been involved in local home school leadership. All of this makes our children prime candidates for "the fishbowl complex." As my husband has chosen to leave the children out of sermon illustrations on Sunday morning, I have chosen to keep anecdotal information regarding my family to a minimum. However, I thought I'd include a little peek at our home before I close.

We live in a small city on a tree lined street. I am awakened in the morning by the sound of a pesky woodpecker drumming on the gutter outside our bedroom window. There are no cows, no goats, or other country experiences. Our livestock is limited to a faithful elderly labrador and a young dwarf lop-eared rabbit appropriately named Sophie the Killer Bunny. Soon Sophie will be moving to a country home where she will earn her keep fertilizing the garden.

Rarely does the smell of fresh bread waft through our house. We are on a first name basis with the manager of the closest pizza carryout. I sew for the younger children for Christmas gifts — maybe. I battle the extra weight put on with my last pregnancy when I was scraping forty. At this point it'll probably never go away. I wear shoes in the kitchen in case I should step on something sticky.

My husband and I have been married almost twenty-four years. They have been years full of happiness and struggle as two flawed people try to learn what it means to become one flesh in all areas of life. We still have a long way to go, but by God's grace we have made progress.

Our children often fill us with joy. They can also fill us with emotions that are not listed under the fruit of the Spirit. As parents striving to grow them up in the Lord, we are growing up ourselves.

In examining our family you will not find any piano virtuosos, National Merit scholars, or entrepreneurs poised to earn their first million by the age of twenty. As spiritual mountaineers, we have not often scaled to giddy heights, but rather find ourselves struggling over the rocks strewn along the pathway to the summit.

In short, we are sinners saved by grace with a glorious future hope. We are joined by a vast company, past, present, and future. Together we look to Jesus, the author and finisher of our faith. As my fellow pilgrims, I hope this book provides practical help for the home school portion of your journey. My prayers go with you, as I hope yours will go with us. The Lord bless you!

Appendix A: Resources

ADDRESSES

Both secular and Christian resources are included, so discretion may be needed to sift out some occasional chaff. On the whole, however, you will find a wealth of helpful information.

COLLEGE INFORMATION

Advanced Placement Classes
www.pahomeschoolers.com

College — general help
www.homeschoolteenscollege.net
(This is Cafi Cohen's site, author of *And What About College?*)

College Search
www.campuslife.net
www.usnews.com
www.petersons.com

College Search — distance learning
www.gospelcom.net/bakersguide/
www.geteducated.com
www.petersons.com
www.worldcampus.psu.edu (Penn State)
www.uiowa.edu (University of Iowa)

College Search — home school friendly schools
www.hslda.org
www.learninfreedom.org

College Testing
ACT: www.act.org
PSAT, SAT, AP, CLEP: www.collegeboard.org

College Financial Aid
FastWeb: www.fastweb.com
Finaid: www.finaid.com

CORRESPONDENCE SCHOOLS AND/OR PUBLISHERS

This list contains address information for major correspondence schools and smaller publishers whose materials are not always widely available through bookstores or home school catalogs. It is not meant to be exhaustive. If my often repeated advice has persuaded you to purchase Cathy Duffy or Mary Prides' books you should find all the address information you need in their publications.

4:20 Communications
P.O. Box 421027
Minneapolis MN 55442-0027
888-420-READ
www.phonicstutor.com

A Beka Book, Inc.
Box 19100
Pensacola, FL 32523-9100
877-223-5226
General Web site: www.abeka.com
Distance Learning: www.abekaacademy.org

Alpha Omega
300 North McKemy Avenue
Chandler, AZ 85226-2618
800-622-3070
Alpha Omega Academy: 800-682-7396
Alpha Omega On-line Academy: 877-688-2652
www.home-schooling.com

American School
2200 E. 170th St.
Lansing, IL 60438
800-531-9268
www.americanschoolofcorr.com

American Textbook Committee
4204 Summerville Road
Phenix City, AL 36867-2130
706-573-3656

American Vision
P.O. Box 220
Powder Springs, GA 30127
800-628-9460
www.avision1.com

Bob Jones University Press, also:
Academy of Home Education
HomeSat
Testing and Evaluation
1700 Wade Hampton Blvd.
Greenville, SC 29614
800-845-5731
www.bjup.com

Cadron Creek Christian Curriculum
4329 Pinos Altos Road
Silver City, NM 88061
www.cadroncreek.com

Canon Press
P.O. Box 8729
Moscow, ID 83843
800-488-2034
www.canonpress.org

Castlemoyle Books
P.O. Box 520
Pomeroy, WA 99347
1-888-773-5586
www.castlemoyle.com

Chalkdust Company
11 Sterling Court
Sugar Land, TX 77479
800-588-7564
www.chalkdust.com

Christian Liberty Academy/Press
502 W. Euclid Ave.
Arlington Heights, IL 60004
Catalog: 800-832-2741
Academy: 800-348-0899
www.homeschools.org

Cornerstone Curriculum Project
2006 Flat Creek
Richardson, TX 75080
972-235-5149
www.cornerstonecurriculum.com

Covenant Home Curriculum
N63 W23421 Main Street
Sussex, WI 53089
800-578-2421
www.educate@covenanthome.com

Covenant Publications
224 Auburn Avenue
Monroe, LA 71201
318-323-3061

Crown Financial Ministries
P.O. Box 2458
Gainesville, GA 30503-2458
800-722-1976
www.crown.org

Eagle Christian High School
888-324-5348
www.eaglechristian.org

Escondido Tutorial Service
2634 Bernardo Ave.
Escondido, CA 92029
760-746-0980
www.gbt.org

FEE (Foundation for Economic Education)
Irvington-on-Hudson, NY 10533
800-452-3518

Institute for Excellence in Writing
P.O. Box 6065
Atascadero, CA 93423
800-856-5815
www.writing-edu.com

Kapco Library Products
1000 Cherry Street
P.O. Box 626
Kent OH, 44240-0011
800-791-8965
www.kapcolibrary.com

Key Curriculum Press
1150 65th Street
Emeryville, CA 94608
800-995-MATH
www.keycurriculumpress.com

Keystone National High School
School House Station
420 West 5th St.
Bloomsburg, PA 17815
800-255-4937
www.keystonehighschool.com

Konos, Inc.
P.O. Box 250
Anna, TX 75409
972-924-2712
www.konos.com

Math U See
www.mathusee.com

Paradigm Company
P.O. Box 45161
Boise, ID 83711
208-322-4440
www.howtotutor.com

Providence Project
14566 NW 110th Street
Whitewater, KS 67154
888-776-8776
www.providenceproject.com

Rod and Staff Publishers, Inc.
P.O. Box 3 Hwy 172
Crockett, KY 41413-0003
606-522-4348

Runkle Publishers
3750 W. Main, 3 Park South
Norman, OK 73072
1-877-436-8398
www.runklepub.com

Schola Publications
1698 Market Street, Suite 162
Redding, CA 96001
916-275-2064

School of Tomorrow
Living Heritage Academy
P.O. Box 299000
Lewisville, TX 75029-9000
800-925-7777
www.schooloftomorrow.com

Scroll Publishing
P.O. Box 6175
Tyler, TX 75711
www.earlychurch.com

SOLA (Scholar's On-line Academy)
520-751-1942
Web site: www.islas.org

Soli Deo Gloria Publications
P.O. Box 451
Morgan, PA 15064
412-221-1901
www.SDGbooks.com

Sonlight Curriculum Ltd.
8042 South Grant Way
Littleton, CO 80122-2705
303-730-6292
www.sonlight.com

CORRESPONDENCE SCHOOLS AND/OR PUBLISHERS (CONT'D)

Steck Vaughn
800-531-5015
www.steck-vaughn.com

The Teaching Company
7405 Alban Station Court
Suite A107
Springfield, VA 22150
800-832-2412
www.teachco.com

Teaching Tape Technology
8648 Hwy 11
Chelsea, AL 35043
205-678-9996
www.teachingtape.com

Texas Tech University
Outreach and Extended Studies
Box 42191
Lubbock, TX 79409-2191
800-692-6877 Ext. 258
www.dce.ttu.edu/

Vic Lockman
233 Rogue River Hwy, #360
Grants Pass, OR 97527
877-208-3366

VideoText Interactive
P.O. Box 19761
Indianapolis, IN 46219
800-254-3272
www.videotext.com

Vision Video
www.visionvideo.com

W.H. Freeman and Company
(Jacobs' math)
www.whfreeman.com

Wordsmith
1355 Ferry Road
Grants Pass, OR 97526
541-476-3080
www.jsgrammar.com

National Organizations

Home School Legal Defense Association
(National Center for Home Education)
P.O. Box 3000
Purcellville, VA 20134
540-338-5600
www.hslda.org

NATHHAN
(National Challenged Homeschoolers Associated Network)
P.O. Box 39
Porthill, ID 83853
208-267-6246
www.NATHHAN.com

Summit Ministries
P.O. Box 207
Manitou Springs, CO 80829
719-685-9103
www.summit.org

Worldview Academy
P.O. Box 310106
New Braunfels, TX 78131
800-241-1123
www.worldview.org

RETAIL AVAILABILITY OF HOME SCHOOL MATERIALS

Homeschool Headquarters
www.homeschoolheadquarters.com

BOOKS ON HOME SCHOOLING HIGH SCHOOLERS

The following three books by Cafi Cohen contain much helpful information. Published by secular publishers, you will find a heavier inclusion of unschooling ideology than is found in publications widely available on the Christian home school market.

Adams-Gordon, Beverly. *Home School, High School, and Beyond*. Pomeroy, WA: Castlemoyle Books, 1999. (A nine week course that involves a teen in planning his high school course of study.)

Cohen, Cafi. *And What About College? 2nd edition*. Cambridge, MA: Holt Associates, 2000. (A helpful biographical presentation of one family's successful road to college admission.)

Cohen, Cafi. *Homeschoolers' College Admissions Handbook*. Roseville, CA: Prima Publishing, 2000. (More advice on college admissions from Cafi Cohen with suggestions from other home schoolers sprinkled liberally throughout.)

Cohen, Cafi. *Homeschooling the Teen Years*. Roseville, CA: Prima Publishing, 2000. (another book full of anecdotal information from many home school families.)

Dennis, Jeanne Gowen. *Homeschooling High School*. Lynnwood, WA: Emerald Books, 2000. (The results of Dennis' extensive college survey on attitudes towards home schoolers, admissions policies, etc. are a unique and helpful feature of this book.)

Duffy, Cathy. *Christian Home Educators' Curriculum Manual: Junior/Senior High*. Westminster, CA: Grove Publishing, 2000. (Cathy Duffy offers correspondence school information, help in planning your school program, and textbook reviews in all subjects with address information for finding the materials reviewed.)

Pride, Mary. *The Big Book of Home Learning, Volume 1: Getting Started* and *Volume 3: Junior High to College*. Chandler, AZ: Alpha Omega Publications, 2000. (Although similar to Cathy Duffy's book, you will find the two authors' books have different personalities, contain different information, and sometimes reach different conclusions. I have found both authors helpful through the years.)

BOOKS FOR PARENTS

Priolo, Lou. *The Heart Of Anger*. New York: Calvary Press, 1997. (Excellent biblical advice on dealing with a child with an angry heart. In the process of seeking help for the child, you'll also find help for the parent!)

Tripp, Paul David. *Age of Opportunity*. Phillipsburg, NJ: P&R Publishing, 1997. (Tripp encourages us to see the teen years as a time of opportunity for spiritual growth in both teen and parent.)

Tripp, Paul David. *War of Words*. Phillipsburg, NJ: P&R Publishing, 1997. (Subtitled "Getting to the Heart of Your Communication Struggles," this excellent book encourages us to examine the heart from which our words spring and our relationship with God and others.)

Appendix B: Forms

The forms in Appendix B are to help you plan and organize your high school course of study.

Feel free to photocopy any of these forms for your personal homeschool.

FOUR YEAR STUDY PLAN FOR _____

9th grade courses	Credit	10th grade courses	Credit
Total		Total	

11th grade courses	Credit	12th grade courses	Credit
Total		Total	

Total Credits by Subject Area

Bible		Computers	
English		Foreign Language	
Math		Fine Arts	
Science		Health and P.E.	
Social Studies		Misc. Electives	

Four Year Total _____

ONE YEAR STUDY PLAN

Name: _____ Grade: _____ Year: _____

Course Title	TEXTS OR MATERIALS

Notes:

PRELIMINARY COURSE CONTRACT	
NAME: SCHOOL YEAR:	
COURSE: CREDIT:	
REQUIREMENTS:	DATE COMPLETED
GRADING METHOD	

COMPLETED COURSE CONTRACT

NAME:	SCHOOL YEAR:
COURSE:	CREDIT:
PARENT'S SIGNATURE:	GRADE:

COURSE DESCRIPTION

CREDITING AND GRADING DATA

GRADE

Criteria	% earned (in decimal form)	x	possible points	% of final grade
			Total %	
			Final Grade	

TIME RECORD #1

NAME: SCHOOL YEAR: COURSE:

HOURS	15 min. div.	BOOK OR ACTIVITY	HOURS	15 min. div.	BOOK OR ACTIVITY
1	☐☐☐☐		31	☐☐☐☐	
2	☐☐☐☐		32	☐☐☐☐	
3	☐☐☐☐		33	☐☐☐☐	
4	☐☐☐☐		34	☐☐☐☐	
5	☐☐☐☐		35	☐☐☐☐	
6	☐☐☐☐		36	☐☐☐☐	
7	☐☐☐☐		37	☐☐☐☐	
8	☐☐☐☐		38	☐☐☐☐	
9	☐☐☐☐		39	☐☐☐☐	
10	☐☐☐☐		40	☐☐☐☐	
11	☐☐☐☐		41	☐☐☐☐	
12	☐☐☐☐		42	☐☐☐☐	
13	☐☐☐☐		43	☐☐☐☐	
14	☐☐☐☐		44	☐☐☐☐	
15	☐☐☐☐		45	☐☐☐☐	
16	☐☐☐☐		46	☐☐☐☐	
17	☐☐☐☐		47	☐☐☐☐	
18	☐☐☐☐		48	☐☐☐☐	
19	☐☐☐☐		49	☐☐☐☐	
20	☐☐☐☐		50	☐☐☐☐	
21	☐☐☐☐		51	☐☐☐☐	
22	☐☐☐☐		52	☐☐☐☐	
23	☐☐☐☐		53	☐☐☐☐	
24	☐☐☐☐		54	☐☐☐☐	
25	☐☐☐☐		55	☐☐☐☐	
26	☐☐☐☐		56	☐☐☐☐	
27	☐☐☐☐		57	☐☐☐☐	
28	☐☐☐☐		58	☐☐☐☐	
29	☐☐☐☐		59	☐☐☐☐	
30	☐☐☐☐		60	☐☐☐☐	

TIME RECORD #2

NAME: SCHOOL YEAR: COURSE:

HOURS	15 min. div.	BOOK OR ACTIVITY	HOURS	15 min. div.	BOOK OR ACTIVITY
61	☐☐☐☐		91	☐☐☐☐	
62	☐☐☐☐		92	☐☐☐☐	
63	☐☐☐☐		93	☐☐☐☐	
64	☐☐☐☐		94	☐☐☐☐	
65	☐☐☐☐		95	☐☐☐☐	
66	☐☐☐☐		96	☐☐☐☐	
67	☐☐☐☐		97	☐☐☐☐	
68	☐☐☐☐		98	☐☐☐☐	
69	☐☐☐☐		99	☐☐☐☐	
70	☐☐☐☐		100	☐☐☐☐	
71	☐☐☐☐		101	☐☐☐☐	
72	☐☐☐☐		102	☐☐☐☐	
73	☐☐☐☐		103	☐☐☐☐	
74	☐☐☐☐		104	☐☐☐☐	
75	☐☐☐☐		105	☐☐☐☐	
76	☐☐☐☐		106	☐☐☐☐	
77	☐☐☐☐		107	☐☐☐☐	
78	☐☐☐☐		108	☐☐☐☐	
79	☐☐☐☐		109	☐☐☐☐	
80	☐☐☐☐		110	☐☐☐☐	
81	☐☐☐☐		111	☐☐☐☐	
82	☐☐☐☐		112	☐☐☐☐	
83	☐☐☐☐		113	☐☐☐☐	
84	☐☐☐☐		114	☐☐☐☐	
85	☐☐☐☐		115	☐☐☐☐	
86	☐☐☐☐		116	☐☐☐☐	
87	☐☐☐☐		117	☐☐☐☐	
88	☐☐☐☐		118	☐☐☐☐	
89	☐☐☐☐		119	☐☐☐☐	
90	☐☐☐☐		120	☐☐☐☐	

TIME RECORD #3

NAME: SCHOOL YEAR: COURSE:

HOURS	15 min. div.	BOOK OR ACTIVITY	HOURS	15 min. div.	BOOK OR ACTIVITY
121	☐☐☐☐		151	☐☐☐☐	
122	☐☐☐☐		152	☐☐☐☐	
123	☐☐☐☐		153	☐☐☐☐	
124	☐☐☐☐		154	☐☐☐☐	
125	☐☐☐☐		155	☐☐☐☐	
126	☐☐☐☐		156	☐☐☐☐	
127	☐☐☐☐		157	☐☐☐☐	
128	☐☐☐☐		158	☐☐☐☐	
129	☐☐☐☐		159	☐☐☐☐	
130	☐☐☐☐		160	☐☐☐☐	
131	☐☐☐☐		161	☐☐☐☐	
132	☐☐☐☐		162	☐☐☐☐	
133	☐☐☐☐		163	☐☐☐☐	
134	☐☐☐☐		164	☐☐☐☐	
135	☐☐☐☐		165	☐☐☐☐	
136	☐☐☐☐		166	☐☐☐☐	
137	☐☐☐☐		167	☐☐☐☐	
138	☐☐☐☐		168	☐☐☐☐	
139	☐☐☐☐		169	☐☐☐☐	
140	☐☐☐☐		170	☐☐☐☐	
141	☐☐☐☐		171	☐☐☐☐	
142	☐☐☐☐		172	☐☐☐☐	
143	☐☐☐☐		173	☐☐☐☐	
144	☐☐☐☐		174	☐☐☐☐	
145	☐☐☐☐		175	☐☐☐☐	
146	☐☐☐☐		176	☐☐☐☐	
147	☐☐☐☐		177	☐☐☐☐	
148	☐☐☐☐		178	☐☐☐☐	
149	☐☐☐☐		179	☐☐☐☐	
150	☐☐☐☐		180	☐☐☐☐	

COMPUTING A GPA

NINTH GRADE				TENTH GRADE			
COURSE	1st semester grade/points	2nd semester grade/points	# of semesters	COURSE	1st semester grade/points	2nd semester grade/points	# of semesters
Total grade points by semester				Total grade points by semester			
Total grade points and semesters				Total grade points and semesters			
Total grade points for year divided by total semesters of class = GPA				Total grade points for year divided by total semesters of class = GPA			

ELEVENTH GRADE				TWELFTH GRADE			
COURSE	1st semester grade/points	2nd semester grade/points	# of semesters	COURSE	1st semester grade/points	2nd semester grade/points	# of semesters
Total grade points by semester				Total grade points by semester			
Total grade points and semesters				Total grade points and semesters			
Total grade points for year divided by total semesters of class = GPA				Total grade points for year divided by total semesters of class = GPA			

Add four yearly grade points together:

Divide total grade points by four to get final grade point average:

FINAL GRADE POINT AVERAGE =

READING LIST	
TITLE	AUTHOR

ACADEMIC TRANSCRIPT RECORD

Name:

Address:

Date of Birth: Sex:

Social Security Number:

Administrator's Signature:

NINTH GRADE					
COURSE	1ST SEM	2ND SEM	FINAL GRADE	CREDIT	

9TH GRADE GPA: 9TH GRADE CREDITS:

ELEVENTH GRADE					

11TH GRADE GPA: 11TH GRADE CREDITS:

One Credit Hour =

School:

Address:

Credits Earned: GPA:

Date of Graduation:

Date Transcript Issued:

Date of College Entry:

TENTH GRADE					
COURSE	1ST SEM	2ND SEM	FINAL GRADE	CREDIT	

10TH GRADE GPA: 10TH GRADE CREDITS:

TWELFTH GRADE					

1ST SEMESTER GPA: 12TH GRADE CREDITS:

Grading Scale:

ACADEMIC TRANSCRIPT RECORD

Name:		School:	
Address:		Address:	
		Credits Earned:	GPA:
Date of Birth:	Sex:	Date of Graduation:	
Social Security Number:		Date Transcript Issued:	
Administrator's Signature:		Date of College Entry:	

Course Name	yr_____9th			yr_____10th			yr_____11th			yr_____12th		
	1st	2nd	Final	1st	2nd	Final	1st	2nd	Final	1st	2nd	Final

One Credit Hour =

Grading Scale: